Growing Up
With Ignorance

Growing Up With Ignorance

Memoirs of a Singaporean Baby Boomer

Lee Ali

PARTRIDGE
A Penguin Random House Company

To order additional copies of this book, contact
Toll Free 800 101 2657 (Singapore)
Toll Free 1 800 81 7340 (Malaysia)
orders.singapore@partridgepublishing.com

www.partridgepublishing.com/singapore

Contents

To Mother and Father,
may you rest in peace.

Acknowledgements

For a long time I toyed with the idea of writing a book about my life. But somehow I kept putting it off. Finally, my son, Kyne told me to get going.

I started with recollections of incidents that occurred. I put my thoughts and analysis alongside each incident. It became quite an unwieldy piece. Kyne told me to please give a clean story line. My son-in-law, Keith gave his views, too. Somehow, the general consensus was a story that flows.

Eva Lim, my wise old friend, felt I should leave the reader to draw conclusions rather than cloud the story with my own biased worldview. With her experience in the educational field and counseling, her guidance has been most valuable. She showed me how the love my 'adopted great grandparents' showered Father counteract the effect from Mother. I am very much indebted to Eva for her valuable insight.

My husband, Ben gave descriptions of places like the three worlds, the scenes in the vicinity of the wayang shows, and how ice-cream was made in those days. The child who spent most of her time within the four walls of a room knew next to nothing of the world outside. His contributions added much color to my descriptions of old Singapore. Thank you dear, for all your support!

Friends marveled at how I could remember so much. Really, painful experiences leave indelible marks. The happier ones, in contrast, became more memorable and valued. Still I relied on my siblings to help make details vivid. Rosie shared her experiences about Father. I believe if she writes her experiences, they will be quite different. Annie mentioned the name Grandmother gave the taxi driver to come to our home. Upon research, I found out

Singapore's one and only mental institution was once near where I lived during those difficult days.

This whole project took me almost two years. I started writing about a year after Mother passed on. My brother, Heng's illness and subsequent demise within two years of Mother's, was an emotionally draining period for all of us. I came to appreciate more my siblings' support for each other. Thank you my dear siblings!

Last but not least, I thank Barbara Schuetz who edited and added clarity to my narration.

Lee Ali

Prologue

Life can only be understood backwards, but it must be lived forwards.

—Kierkegaard

This is a subjective account of my growing up in the early years of emerging Singapore. Those were the days when many parents had little or no education. They relied on what they learned from their parents or heard from others to raise their offspring. I guess my parents were no different. They did their best, struggling with impoverished resources.

But whatever parents did had profound effects on their children. Some children would do well, some not so well but could get by, while some ended up in institutions. And it was often those who led illustrious or notorious lives who came to media attention. But what happened to the rest may be worth knowing—the suffering that was unknowingly inflicted was often sustained through their whole lives. Let the mistakes made be known, and the hurt and suffering, too, so that our uneducated parents did not live in vain.

All accounts related happened and the places described or mentioned existed. But some places have long since given way to development. As these places and foods related to an era of old, I have used their old names—the way Mother would say them in the Hokkien dialect.

I have also used my siblings' real names. We are a simple lot with nothing to hide. As for other persons, their names have been changed to protect their identities. Most were substituted with English names to make reading easier.

Lee Ali
(Ali, as my parents and grandparents called me.)

Chapter 1

Mother's Origin

Little is actually known about Mother's biological ancestors.

Great-Grandmother adopted four children, two boys and two girls. Then she paired them up and had them married. So Grandfather and Grandmother were adopted as brother and sister. Mother was the firstborn of this union.

There was never any mention of Great-Grandfather. Did he exist? Or was Great-Grandmother single? Nevertheless, Great-Grandmother was the matriarch and tyrant in that household. She disciplined by inflicting physical pain. Grandmother used to tell stories of being chased and beaten by her.

Grandmother appeared to be the least favored of Great-Grandmother's four children.

The relationship among the four adopted siblings appeared cool. I never saw Grandfather meet with his brother. Grandmother was often lukewarm toward her sister, Third- Grandaunt. She said Great-Grandmother favored Third-Grandaunt. Third-Grandaunt was allowed to attend school, while the others were not. But Third-Grandaunt played truant and dropped out of school very early. So, all four children were quite illiterate.

Third-Grandaunt had a tough life. Third-Granduncle, her husband, was in and out of mental institutions. During the days, when he was more functional, he worked as a trishaw rider. Third-Grandaunt had to work as an odd-job laborer to supplement his income. It was heavy work, transferring goods from ships' holds to barges or from barges to warehouses. When no ship came into the harbor, Third-Grandaunt often ended up at construction sites, carrying loads of stones and sand. Nevertheless, they brought up a brood of children. The eldest son was educationally subnormal, and two other children were frequently institutionalized because of mental disorders.

When I knew more about heredity, I was quite glad Great-Grandmother did a good job pairing up Grandfather and Grandmother.

My grandparents were not exactly warm to one another. Still, they produced five girls and four boys. Grandmother had married very young. When her daughters and daughter-in-law were giving birth to children, Grandmother was still having babies. No wonder, she was in the early half of her thirties when I was born. So I had one auntie eight months older than me and two younger aunties, not to mention those much older.

There was a big generation gap between Mother and her younger sisters, and that did not bode well for her. The younger siblings resented her bossiness and often had lots to say about her.

Grandfather worked as a port supervisor with the Singapore Harbor Board. He had a team of port workers who respected him a great deal. And he took great care of them.

Every seventh month, Grandfather would make offerings of cooked ducks, chickens, fruits, and cakes to the hungry ghosts[1]. After the prayer, Grandmother would divide the food into portions and have them distributed to Grandfather's colleagues. In this way, Grandmother supported Grandfather pretty well.

Then, during the dumpling festival, Grandmother would wrap large quantities of bak-chung[2] and have them distributed to Grandfather's colleagues. She was a great

---

[1] The seventh month of the lunar year is called the month of the hungry ghosts. During this month, offerings are made to the dead.

[2] Bak-chung is a rice dumpling wrapped in bamboo leaves. The fillings were usually an assortment of meat, mushrooms, chestnuts, dried prawns, and other goodies.

cook. Her ang ku kueh[3] filled with black sesame paste, was superb and yummy.

Grandmother was a homemaker throughout her life. She did not need to leave home to earn a living. When she was in need of cash, she would ask Grandfather. He was not exactly generous with her, but he did provide enough. Sometimes, in her frustration, I heard Grandmother call Grandfather "Lou-au-kui."[4] I was amused. When you are a Lou-au-kui, it means your wife has been sleeping with other men. Grandmother just did not grasp the implication of her words!

In my younger days, when I was allowed to stay with my grandparents for a few days, I noticed Grandfather would take his dinner, enjoy his opium smoking under the big brass bed, and then disappear for the rest of the night. By that time, opium possession had

---

[3]   Glutinous rice cakes filled with peanut or bean paste.
[4]   Literally translated, it means "old tortoise."

become illegal. That's why Grandfather hid under the bed to smoke it.

The place where they were living was one of many rooms in a building specially built to house port workers' families. Grandfather had a separate bed in another building within walking distance from home. That building served as a dormitory for port workers who were single or without families. Grandfather appeared privileged, with a home and also privacy from the growing brood of children.

Being the first grandchild, Mother was not spared the harsh discipline of her grandmother. From a young age, she had to do housework, carrying water from public taps and selling loads of rambutan[5] in the marketplace. For Mother, physical force was a way of discipline. She used it on her younger siblings, too. Grandfather let her be. She was his firstborn, and he loved her dearly. As for Grandmother,

---

[5]   A tropical fruit with thick hairy skin

she had no power against the matriarch—
mother or mother-in-law?

In 1942, when the Japanese invaded
Singapore, Mother was just twelve years old.
It was probably her puberty period. To protect
her from the ruthless Japanese soldiers, her
parents dressed her up like an old woman and
hid her at home. But life was hard; they needed
food. So eventually Mother went to work in the
factories—dressed like an old woman.

Many innocent men were rounded up by
the Japanese and shot dead. Horror stories
like this went around, and Grandfather was
so terrified that he dared not leave home. So
while the ladies ventured out to work, he hid
under the bed.

Years later, whenever there were any
obstacles in our way, Mother would say, "What
is so bad? During the Japanese occupation,
when the streets were dark, I walked alone."
Was Mother hardened by her grandmother
or the atrocities she witnessed during the

Japanese occupation? Your guess is as good as mine. But the harsh wave of discipline certainly swept down the generations.

My very first memory was Mother spanking me for stepping into a puddle of mud. I was quite tiny then, unable to tell right from wrong, good from bad. I had no words to describe feelings yet—无語問苍天.[6] But the pain and several similar incidents embedded the memory of physical assaults in my mind—so much so that I startle whenever there is a sudden movement or somebody suddenly raises an arm.

---

[6]   No speech to ask heaven why.

Chapter 2

Father

If little was known about Mother's biological ancestors, there is practically nothing known about Father's ancestors.

An old couple lost one of their sons through death. He was a young man and just married. One day, while playing cards with his friends, he suddenly collapsed and passed on, leaving no offspring to carry on the family name or provide for his afterlife. So this couple bought a baby boy, my father, in the hope he would pray and make offerings to their dead son during occasions like his death anniversary, birthday, and festive occasions. They were so grateful to have the baby that they named him Tian Sang. It means a gift from heaven.

According to older neighbors, the baby boy came in a basket. Nobody could tell whether he was thoroughbred Chinese or of mixed Asian race. But he looked Chinese enough. In fact, Father was really good-looking, the most handsome man in my life!

During his early childhood days, the old couple doted on Father. They even had a male servant to follow him about and care for him. But they passed on when Father was about eight years old. Left to the care of uncles and aunties, Father eventually had to drop out of primary school to earn his own keep. It seemed the old couple owned several properties, but Father received no share of their estate. So life became hard for this once sheltered boy.

Father worked as a shop assistant and then as a helper at food stalls. Sometimes, when hungry, he would steal tong chye[7] from the shop to eat. He must have eaten too much of

---

7   A preserved vegetable—it is rather salty.

it, because in our family, we were forbidden to add tong chye to our dishes.

Eventually Father got a job with the Health Services Department as an attendant in government clinics, and the General Hospital in Singapore.

Father got along well with his cousins, uncles, and aunties. It seemed he was closest to his eldest uncle's wife and treated her almost like his mother. He told me to call her Popo. But Popo did not live long; I was about four years old, when she had a heart attack and passed on.

Mother did not like Father's relatives. To keep the peace, he gradually distanced himself from them and met up only on special occasions like Chinese New Year.

I often wonder why Father chose Mother. In those days, marriages were mostly arranged.

Not long after the Japanese left Singapore, a matchmaker, on Father's behalf, approached my grandparents. Father was ten years older than Mother and rather late for marriage. (He was twenty-eight years old when I was born.) My grandparents did not object, Mother agreed, and so they married.

Father was really poor. He could not afford to engage a photographer for his wedding. So we had no photographs at all of the wedding.

For a short while, Father and Mother stayed with Popo but eventually moved to a rented room above a Chinese medical store, a short distance from my grandparents' place.

Father got along famously with my grandparents. Grandfather often asked Father to run errands for him. Whenever Grandfather received letters or notices, he would consult Father. At that time, Mother's siblings were as illiterate as their parents. They could neither read English nor Chinese. Father, therefore, became a valued member in the extended family as he could read some English. Grandfather loved him very much, too.

In fact, Grandfather was closer to Father than to any of his own sons.

Father was also handy. He moved about on his bicycle. Whenever he found electrical appliances or big pieces of wood that were discarded, he would bring them home. He repaired the appliances and made them as good as new for our own use. He sawed and pieced together the odd pieces of wood he found into furniture. We were really too poor to buy our own. So what Father made was really useful. He was a frugal man—he left nothing to waste.

I can still remember the cabinet Father made from door panels of some glass windows. It was so transparent that Mother sewed curtains to hang on the inside. The curtains were plastic sheets with colorful pictures of fishes. The net result: a cabinet that looked like an aquarium! Nonetheless the cabinet served us for many years.

Father seemed to have a knack for such handiwork. He was never formally instructed on electrical wiring or carpentry. But he picked up these skills on his own. Neighbors often asked him to fix their broken electric kettles or irons. He always obliged and never asked for anything in return. So he was popular among the neighbors.

It would appear that Mother caught the most popular man in the neighborhood. But she gradually became dissatisfied with him.

For one thing, he was stuck in his job and never progressed. The pay was low. In those days, some men who were just as lowly educated as Father could get jobs tallying goods on the ships that arrived in the harbor. They earned better money, and some even rose to higher positions. But Father didn't seem to have the courage to try.

He learned to make delicacies like ngoh-hiang[8] and Hokkien[9] prawn noodles while

---

[8]   Meat rolls

[9]   A Chinese dialect commonly spoken in Singapore, the Hokkiens were the majority among the Chinese in Singapore.

helping out at the food stalls. They were pretty delicious. Mother felt he could have ventured into the food business and made more money. In fact, those stalls that he worked for actually became very popular and well known. Again, Father just did not want to do that.

So it was quite frustrating for Mother.

The sorest bone of contention was Father's obsession to provide for his adopted dead ancestors.

In our family home, a black-and-white portrait of a young man wearing a hat and a shirt with Mandarin collar sat on the altar. The face was expressionless. He was the adopted father that Father never really knew. Every evening, joss sticks were burned for him. On his death and birth anniversaries, offerings of food were made in addition to burning paper money. Father insisted on having fried noodles, yam, poultry, fruits, and soup. It was always a grand meal that was too much to consume and food had to be thrown away.

As if that was not enough, Father also made similar offerings to his adopted grandparents. One of the anniversaries fell three days before Chinese New Year's Eve. The need to repeat offerings within a short period really left big holes in the family pocket. Of course, often after such offerings, Mother found herself short of cash. Father could not produce more. So Mother would kick up a big fuss. Scenes like this, so frequently enacted, simply drove me crazy.

Chapter 3

My Earliest Recollections

My earliest recollections date back to life in the rented room above the medical store. My parents never told me when I started talking or walking. I guess memories can only be created when there is enough vocabulary to record events in our minds. So I really cannot recall my toddler days.

That room above the medical store belonged to the store owner, Ah Peh. I was probably about three years old or older then. I do remember the few occasions when Mother touched my forehead and announced, "You have a fever. Go downstairs and get a leng-liang[10] drink

---

[10]   Scrapings from the rhino's horn

from Ah Peh." I would obediently carry the tin cup and money she gave me and walk down the stairs. Then I waited patiently as Ah Peh ground a rhino horn with a stone grinder and water. When there was enough, he poured the contents into my tin cup. I would gulp down the contents. "Ugh!" It tasted odd. But I downed every drop.

By that tender age, I was already conditioned not to defy Mother's orders, and I was quite obedient. How she did it beats me now!

But then was Mother ever satisfied with me? No! There was Rosie. She was two years younger than me. She cried whenever she lost sight of Mother. Mother would say, "Asi has a heart for me." She meant Rosie loved her. As for me, interested in play and not bothered when Mother was out of sight, she said, "Ali has no heart for me at all!" And for years I heard this frequent complaint. Mother told everyone—her parents, siblings, friends, and relatives. But she never taught me how to cultivate a heart for her.

I was my parents' firstborn. If Father was disappointed I was a girl, he never showed it. Much later I overheard Mother tell a neighbor that Great-Grandmother urged Father to give me away. That upset him so much that he quarreled with the old woman. Yes, Father had the duty to carry on the family name so he needed a son, not a daughter. But I was his first blood relative; it would be hard to part with me.

As for Great-Grandmother, she never visited after that. When she passed on, I was an infant so I never got to know her.

Father doted on me. He made a perch on his bicycle especially for me. Whenever he was off work, we would go cycling around the neighborhood. Often we ended up at Ah Bie's place. Ah Bie was one of Father's six blood brothers[11] and his best friend, too.

---

[11] In those days, the Chinese liked to form brotherhoods with friends. They went through a ceremony of dripping blood into cups of wine and swore loyalty to each other.

Well, Ah Bie's place was a farm. His parents lived there with him. They reared many chickens and ducks. The hens seemed to produce lots of eggs. Ah Bie's mother frequently served us mugs of hot Milo[12] drinks each flavored with an egg. I loved to see the bright orange yolk floating on the top of the drink. One day, there was no egg in my drink!

"Hee, hee, hee, Ali is very smart. No egg in her Milo, so she is not going to Ah Bie's place anymore," I later overheard Father telling Mother.

---

[12] A mixture of chocolate and malt powder

Chapter 4

The Cabin above the Garage

I was probably about three and a half years old when Father was transferred to work in a dispensary in Oukang,[13] quite far away from the General Hospital and the area around the harbor where Grandfather worked. So we had to move.

The new place was a small cabin above the dispensary's garage. There was no toilet, no bathroom, and no kitchen. A flight of stairs led us down to the dispensary's bathroom and public toilet. The space outside the cabin door was the flat roof of the toilet and bathroom. It was sheltered. Two sides had railings to

---

13   Old name of a place in Singapore's Paya Lebar district

protect us children from falling off. At the far end facing the cabin was the sloping tiled roof of the caretaker's kitchen. The dispensary's caretaker appeared to be much higher in rank than Father. His family enjoyed much better equipped and more comfortable accommodations.

Father was very innovative. He made a sink for Mother out of an old dustbin cover. Then he perched a huge tin can above this sink, installing a tap just above it. He used a rubber hose to siphon water from the bathroom below into the tin can. So, lo and behold, we had our own quaint-looking kitchen sink!

The space outside the cabin was big enough for Mother to cook and for us children to play. In fact we spent most of our waking hours there.

Life was hard with Father's meager income. Far away from her parents, Mother had less support. On a few occasions, she pawned personal items like her brass belt to buy food for the family.

Eventually, my parents found a way to make extra money. In those days, there were no plastic bottles. Patients often needed extra containers for their medication. So Father obtained small bottles from rag-and-bone men. These bottles were quite dirty. Mother would help him wash and dry them. Father then sold the bottles to the patients. This worked out fine. In fact some patients even tipped Father for his efforts.

Life, then, would have been idyllic for this young couple, but Mother often fell sick. Every time it was a problem with her menstruation, and she had to be hospitalized for a "wash." As there was no one to take care of Rosie and me, Father and Grandmother would bring us along when they visited Mother. But the hospital refused to let children into the wards. So Rosie and I would be left sitting in the lobby. Rosie would cry nonstop. It was really awful for me. But Mother was pleased when she learned of it. "Asi has a heart for me; Ali is useless, and she has no heart for me at all." That was her usual refrain.

On normal days, when Father was out working, Mother had no help. She had to buy food and necessities. So Mother would leave Rosie and me behind. Rosie would cry and cry until Mother returned. I couldn't do much with her. Sometimes it was so awful that I cried, too.

Mother became upset when she got home. She took out her cane and whipped us both. As she did so, she demanded, "Say you will not do it again!" I refused to do just that. She beat me even harder. My fingers became sore trying to ward off the cane. Deep cane marks appeared all over my body and limbs. "Don't ever say sorry," I told myself as the cane rained over me.

In contrast to Mother, Father was a much gentler parent. Even when frustrated he never laid his hands on us. Once he was so upset with Rosie's nonstop crying that he threw away her milk and made her drink black coffee from her bottle instead. After that, Mother liked to joke about this.

Chapter 5

Time with My Grandparents

Home was a long way from my grandparents', a long tram ride from Oukang to Kampong Bahru[14] and then a bus ride. In those days, tramcars were the most prevalent transport. The skyline was filled with unwieldy electric cables crisscrossing all over. It was a very confusing world to me.

By the time we reached our grandparents' home, Mother was in a foul mood. Fetching two small children and traversing across Singapore like that was too much for her.

---

14 A district in Singapore

For me, it was always a relief to finally arrive. There were so many more people to play with—and less contact with Mother.

While Rosie clung to her, I would run all over the place with my aunties and play make-believe with whatever objects we could lay our hands on. In those days, toys were scarce.

My playful attitude seemed to anger Mother. She chided me all the more.

The place where my grandparents lived was called the Twenty Rooms. There were exactly twenty rooms, one for each port worker's family. At each end of the building were a common kitchen, toilet, and bathroom. Every room faced the common courtyard that was protected by a brick wall. My grandparents' room was just beside a common bathroom and the nearest to the kitchen.

Outside the Twenty Rooms was a big field. During festive occasions, like the hungry ghosts' month or a god's birthday, there were wayang shows[15]. Raised platforms were erected and allocated to each of the twenty families, so they could get a better view of the show on a raised stage. Grandmother enjoyed the opera very much, but Mother disliked the noise. So she would stay away from such events.

The evening show usually started at seven o'clock and ended at eleven. With her weak legs, Grandmother would still clamber up the raised platform and sit through the whole evening watching the opera. The next day she would be there again. This was life's simple joy for her.

Grandfather had no patience to sit and watch the opera. But he would come and take the aunties and me to the food stalls. There was so much to choose from: rojak,[16] ice balls,

---

[15] Chinese opera

[16] Malay salad comprising of vegetables, bean sprouts, bean curd, and pineapple and topped with gravy made of prawn paste, ground chilies, peanuts, and tamarind juice.

kang kong cuttlefish,[17] fried Hokkien noodles (all local specialties and favorites), whichever I fancied.

In those days, whenever there was a wayang show, besides food, there were also gaming stalls nearby. Games, such as Tikam-Tikam,[18] shooting, and carom, were common. For a small price, you got a chance to win prizes like plastic toys or sweets.

We usually stayed up till the show was over. Life was so much more fun away from Mother!

My grandparents would find every opportunity to get me to stay with them. Mother would grudgingly give her permission, grumbling that I didn't "have her heart" anyway.

---

[17] Local dish containing dark leafy vegetables and dried squid, seasoned with sweet gravy.

[18] Lottery envelopes—the buyer immediately tore open the envelope to find out and claim his prize.

My grandparents showered me with much love and affection. All my young aunties had to give in to me.

I was their first grandchild. Although my grandparents seemed quite indifferent to one another, they shared a common bond over me. To them, I was bright and clever. A neighbor actually pronounced quite insensitively, "She is the ugliest baby I have ever seen." That did not matter to them at all.

Grandfather smoked opium under Grandmother's big brass bed. Wooden blocks supported the four legs giving more height so he could comfortably roast the opium over a flame.

Wafts of aromatic opium filled the air. The flame danced steadily within the glass casing of the burner while Grandfather luxuriated in his one and only vice: smoking.

I liked to sit under the bed with Grandfather and watch him do this. I chattered incessantly, and he would indulgently encourage me to talk nonsense. The aroma of opium lingering in the air was heavenly. To this day, the memory of that smell stays with me.

As he smoked, Ong Toh's voice from the Redifusion[19] came over the airwaves. It was nine o'clock in the evening. Ong Toh told his never-ending kungfu[20] story. The neighbors in the other rooms sat entranced as Ong Toh hypnotized them with visions of their favorite heroes.

Next morning, they gathered in the courtyard. Still filled with visions of the story, they compared notes. They discussed, argued, and debated over what they heard the night before.

---

[19] Redifusion was the only cabled radio broadcast available at that time. Most families would pay a small monthly subscription to get a whole day of entertainment—songs, drama, stories, and news.

[20] Chinese martial arts

Occasionally, someone would say, "What's the name of that...?" Or "He did..." and another would refute, "No, he did..."

I would interject, "His name was...," or "He did..."

They would gasp. "How can this child remember so much?" they wondered aloud.

My grandparents were thrilled with me.

At that tender age, details like this came easily into my consciousness. I just said what came to me without any deliberation. Pure innocence. I knew nothing about propriety. Mother would have chided me for interrupting adult conversations. But, when she was not around, there was no inhibition in me.

There were a few major annual festivals that kept Grandmother very busy. At the start of the lunar year, there was the great prayer to the God of Heaven. The dumpling festival was during the fifth lunar month, the seventh month was for the hungry ghosts, the festival of the moon was in the eighth month, and the pilgrimage to nearby Kusu Island came during the ninth month. Grandmother did much of the cooking. The day before an event, she would make rice cakes and steamed puddings, and slaughter chickens and ducks. Third-Auntie was her regular helper.

Outside the room was a big stone grinder for grinding rice or beans into fine powder. The base was a cylindrical stone about one and a half feet in diameter. It was made of granite. Another cylindrical granite stone about one foot in diameter sat on top of this base. A center pin aligned and secured the top to the base. Third-Auntie used a long, wooden T-shaped handle to work it. This T-shape handle was attached to the side of the top stone. It was tied to the ceiling with ropes. Each time she had to use it, Third-Auntie would lower the handle to waist level and fix the end of the T to the grinder. Then she would spoon soaked glutinous rice or beans into a hole in the top stone. She pushed the handle to rotate the top stone over the bigger stone below. The finely ground rice or beans would drop through a spout into a pot placed just below the grinder. It was hard work. But it seems this was the only grinder in the Twenty Rooms, and it belonged to Grandmother. So the neighbors often would ask to use it. On festive occasions, the stone grinder was worked hard!

Sometimes Mother would go over to help Grandmother. But, unless she could not help it, Mother preferred not to stay overnight. The room was cramped, and most of us children slept on the hard floor or on Grandmother's hard brass bed. There were no mattresses, only straw mats.

While the adults were busy, I joined the younger aunties in their play. We played around the compounds of the Twenty Rooms and in the big field, pulling grass and plucking wild flowers. There was so much life here. There were also chickens and ducks in the courtyard. To save money, Grandmother bought newborn chicks and ducklings to rear. This way she could spend less on those festive prayers. The aunties and I often dug into the earth to find earthworms to feed the poultry.

At the end of the day, when all was done, Father would come and fetch us home. He would whistle to Rosie and me, and we would run into his arms. Father was really dear to me, my only loving parent. The whistle was so special, sharp and distinctly his. Grandmother often jokingly announced, "The big rat is here." Sadly I don't have such fond memories of Mother.

Chapter 6

Those Cabin Days

My parents were a young couple, trying their best to keep their home afloat. Entertainment options in those days were few and far between. A movie theater somewhere down the road featured Hindu shows for fifty cents a seat. The young couple would go there with two small children in tow. Rosie and I squeezed between their seats while they watched and enjoyed the show.

The black-and-white films featured celluloid scenes of kings and princes fighting. In a few shows, someone was beheaded. The strange thing was someone else presented the head to some mighty king and the head talked! I always had nightmares after the shows.

Mother refused to let anyone share her double bed, so Father slept on the floor with one child on each side. On stormy nights, with thunder and lightning, heavy rain pounded the roof. We clung to Father. He would draw us closer to him with his reassuring hands.

Nightmares drove me to draw even closer to Father. I probably screamed. He used to tell me, "You talk in your sleep."

And Rosie sleepwalked.

Rosie and I had no other playmates. On lazy afternoons, we played quietly in the "kitchen" while Mother slept in the cabin.

Rainwater dripped from the slope of the caretaker's kitchen. I often caught ants, put them into the water, and watched them swim.

I can never remember any conversations with Rosie. We played quietly side by side, not making much noise in case the ruckus induced a beating from Mother.

After her nap, Mother would give us each a cup of light black coffee and two pieces of biscuits. They were cheap ones, bought by weight to feed the whole family—small square crackers, Marie biscuits, or small round biscuits with pink, green, or white icing candies stuck to them. Fruits were luxuries and appeared only when there was an offering to the gods or ancestors.

Down the road was the Temple of the Ninth God. Every year on the ninth month, from the first to the ninth day, devotees came to offer prayers. Before coming, they had to abstain from fish or meat from the start of the day.

This was a business time for vendors, who sold their wares on pushcarts around the temple. Odd things, like black beetles strung on sticks, lay sumptuously on trays ready for consumption. There was food galore and wayang shows throughout the period.

At the end of the day, one or two fruit vendors would leave their heavy carts within the gates of the dispensary—right under our cabin. These vendors would occasionally pass a fruit or two to my parents. Being the only attendant in the dispensary, and with his helpful disposition, Father was well liked among the locals in the vicinity.

The neighborhood around the Temple of the Ninth God bustled with activities. But I never had the chance to venture out. Mother held such a tight grip on me that for a long time I did not know how to go places on my own.

Father planted bananas in the backyard of the dispensary. I watched in awe the first time he cut a big bunch from the plant, separated the fruit into combs, and distributed them to friends and neighbors.

The caretaker's family also reared chickens in the backyard. One night, when they were entertaining friends and playing mahjong, someone shouted, "Chicken thieves!" Everyone scrambled into the dark. Someone was trying to get over the wall. Someone else caught hold of a leg, pulled the person down, and landed a punch. Only to find out later, he was one of them!

These were fun if not sweet memories of that little cabin. A lonely childhood could only rely on such episodes to spice up life.

Chapter 7

Godparents and Beliefs

My parents were worried about Rosie's frequent crying. They consulted a temple medium. The medium advised them to find a set of godparents for her. Eventually, they found our former neighbors, a couple who had lived above the medical store. They had several children. One requirement for Rosie's development was a complete family with a big brood of children.

Rosie's new godparents were excited. They bought clothes and toys for her, and bowls and chopsticks, too. On "adoption" day, we went to their house so Rosie could pay respect to their ancestors. By now they had moved to a flat in the Silat[21] area. Thereafter, on major festive occasions like the moon festival and Lunar New Year, the godparents would buy Rosie gifts and clothes. On important occasions, we would go to their house for dinner. The second day of the Lunar New Year was a big affair for them—they "opened" the year with prayers to the gods and ancestors, and then a reunion meal.

The dresses Rosie received were often too big, so I wore them instead. She also received a tricycle that we took turns riding around the "kitchen."

It suddenly occurred in my innocent mind, "How is it I have no godparents?"

"Why is it I have no godparents?" I asked Mother.

"Yes, you have. You were so hard to bring up, with so many illnesses and diarrhea. The

---

[21]   Another district in Singapore

gods said you could not be too close to your parents—that's why you call us Ah Chek and Ah Chim.[22] We asked around, but nobody wanted to be your godparents. Finally I offered chicken and roast pork to the Kitchen God and told him you were his godchild. Incidentally, you were born on the day he went to heaven to report on everybody's behavior."

Wow! When mortals reject, immortals had to accept. Lo and behold, I had a *God* parent!

Meanwhile, the little child that was me waited in vain for the Kitchen God to send me a gift.

Mother faithfully observed the birthday of the Kitchen God. Every year, without fail, she would offer chicken and roast pork among other things to the Kitchen God.

One thing Mother had in common with Grandmother was praying. They often went

---

[22] Auntie and Uncle

to the temples to pray to Guan Yin[23] and Tua Peh Kong.[24] Then, during the ninth month, they would make a pilgrimage to Kusu Island.

Going to Kusu Island seemed a big affair, too. Grandmother would cook yellow rice and decorate it all over with boiled prawns. Mother and Father would go with her, and they brought Rosie along. I was left behind to play with the aunties.

Kusu Island was a small island a short distance from the southern part of Singapore. In those days, only tongkangs[25] plied from Clifford Pier to this island. During the ninth month, the tongkangs would be very crowded. Mother found it troublesome to bring me along. So I had no chance to visit the island until much later in life. I heard Mother talk about it though. Besides the Chinese temple, there was also a Hindu temple on the only small hill. My

---

[23] Goddess of Mercy
[24] The Big God
[25] Chinese bumboats, without engines, needed to be rowed.

parents and Grandmother would pray to both the Chinese and Hindu gods there.

It was unclear what their religion was. Mother and Father claimed to be Buddhists, but they went to Taoist temples. They even prayed to Hindu gods. It seemed to me whenever and wherever there was a god, they would pray to them.

The temple medium was another source of comfort for them. Whenever there was a problem or sickness, Mother would go with Grandmother to consult a medium. I used to get frightened by the sight of the medium going into a trance and acting strangely. But they had faith in such things. Sometimes, they even went to one to "talk" to a dead ancestor!

Chapter 8

Marriages of Mother's Siblings

Being the eldest, Mother was involved in all matters related to her family, from her siblings' marriages to family problems to sickness.

Second-Uncle reached marriageable age. Being a port worker and uneducated, he had no chance to meet a woman on his own. So my grandparents had to arrange his marriage. They looked around for a good match. Eventually, Father spoke to some patients he befriended at the dispensary. Somebody recommended a girl.

In those days, there were three amusement parks in Singapore: the Great World, the New World, and the Happy World. Each one had its own uniqueness.

New World was famous for its dance halls and live shows. For a fee you could choose a partner to dance with. The Joget[26] was a hit then.

Happy World held boxing matches. Boxers from the region—Malaya, Indonesia and Philippines—would come to compete. Badminton competitions were also regularly held there.

Great World was where all the gaming and entertainment were housed. It was an ideal place to meet and socialize. In those days, besides coffee shops and restaurants, there were no other venues suitable to introduce couples to one another. So an arrangement was made for Second-Uncle to meet a girl at Great World. It was an exciting affair.

As usual, Mother was involved and had lots to say before and after the meeting.

When the couple met, it was not love at first sight. Both needed some persuading before

---

[26] Malay social dance

they finally agreed to marry one another. That was it—no dating at all! So preparation for the big day began in earnest.

Mother helped secure items for the gift exchange, plan the dinner menu, rent a room for the couple above the medical store, and much more. I simply loved the times when she was too busy to bother me. And I could spend more time at my grandparents' place.

Eventually the great day arrived. The dinner was held in the courtyard of the Twenty Rooms. Next day, there were pots of leftover food all mixed in a potpourri. We consumed them with relish. They were so much tastier than the original dishes. Neighbors came with tin carriers to scoop from the large pots. It was really fun!

As the eldest in her family, Mother took it upon herself to be present and help on all matters. Be it her siblings' marriages or when they get into trouble with the law, she would rally around. Those closer to her age gave her due respect and listened to her. Later on, the younger ones, who were closer to my age or even younger, resented her bossiness. And Mother was most disapproving of them, too.

As Rosie and I grew up, Mother expected us to be involved in our family matters, too. When relatives visited, I would put down whatever I was doing, get them seated, and serve drinks. I was also expected to make small talk when Mother and Father were not ready to entertain the guests. But Mother still believed children should be seen and not heard, so she would admonish me when I inadvertently joined in their conversations.

That was quite easy for me. But when the younger siblings got into trouble in school, I had to meet the teachers and principals, too. Once, during my late adolescence, I went to meet my brother's form teacher and school principal. After all their talk about the incident, both still insisted on seeing my parents. Father went and came back angry. They complained about Heng (my brother) making obscene signs.

Not long after Second-Uncle's wedding, the family received a proposal for Third-Auntie. The suitor was a young man who worked as a bus conductor with the Singapore Traction Company. At first, Grandfather was against the marriage—the man was from a Teochew[27] family, not Hokkien. Eventually he consented after much persuasion.

I was about two years older than I was during Second-Uncle's wedding. So I could understand what was going on in the whole process of marriage making. First there was haggling over gifts of exchange—matters like candies for grandmothers and shoes for the parents. Then demands were made for ang pow[28] for every member of the family.

Two weeks before the wedding was the day for Guo Da Li.[29] Third-Auntie had a whole trousseau of brand-new samfoo[30] laid out

---

27   A Chinese dialect
28   Red packet containing money as a gift
29   The Great Gift Exchange
30   Sexy pant suits with Mandarin collars

beautifully in a glass cabinet. The samfoo had high Mandarin collars and looked pretty sexy. I was dying to try one on. Grandmother also bought items for Third-Auntie's bridal room—a blanket, bedsheets, pillows, a washbasin, and a chamber pot. The groom's mother prepared and had all the agreed items of the exchange sent over—liquor, pig trotter, oranges, candied peanuts and sweets wrapped in red packets, and most important of all, a set of gold jewelry for Third-Auntie.

The wedding day was eventful. By then, the Harbor Board had allocated a small flat for Grandfather's family. It was on the ground floor of another building not far from Twenty Rooms. At least there was a living room, a bedroom, a kitchen, toilet, bathroom, and a veranda. On the eve, all of us squeezed into the flat and stayed overnight. Squeezed or not, we were excited and did not sleep much.

In accordance with the Teochew custom, the groom must fetch the bride home before the break of dawn. There was much hustle and bustle as the matchmaker accounted for the gifts from the groom's family. Evidently, some items were missing, and there was much arguing. In the process, the bridal party inadvertently left her behind as it hurried off before the sun rose. So, there was a lot of laughter and joking about the matchmaker, making the occasion most memorable.

Second-Auntie made her appearance after Third-Auntie was married. It was then I learned that Third-Auntie had actually been adopted by my grandparents. The story went that Grandmother's legs became very weak after she delivered Second-Auntie. She could not care for Second-Auntie and had to give her away. But later, when Grandmother recovered, she was so guilt-stricken that she adopted another child, Third-Auntie. Third-Auntie was very close to Grandmother. As far as I know she did not attempt to trace or re-unite with her own biological parents.

Second-Auntie's adopted mother passed away early and she had to contend with a stepmother. It seemed her relationship with her adopted father and stepmother was not close. Anyway, they married her off to a young businessman.

After her marriage, she located my grandparents—her biological parents. Of course, Grandmother was thrilled when Second-Auntie returned to her fold! Together, Mother, Second-Auntie, and Third-Auntie became close. They met and visited each other often. At that time, Mother was in her twenties—it was great to have sisters her age to share experiences and thoughts. Then babies were in the making, so everyone seemed very busy.

Well, that was a period of great productivity. About fourteen years later, when Grandfather passed on, there were about twenty grandchildren. It was a big funeral procession when all his children and in-laws lined up. To the Chinese, it meant he had led a good life.

As for Grandmother, more children married and more grandchildren were produced. So, when she passed on thirty years after Grandfather, the funeral procession was twice as long!

Chapter 9

Birth of My Siblings

I was not the first to be conceived. According to Mother, she had a miscarriage before me. It seemed the fetus was well formed by then, and they could tell it was a boy. It must have been quite a blow for Father. He always wanted a son to carry on his family name.

In those days, there was no birth control. My family was really poor and often could not afford to feed another mouth. Yet Mother kept conceiving. The child after me was another girl, Nancy, born in the year of the tiger and at twelve midnight. That was the time when tigers prowl the forest and pounce on their prey. So they believed it was not auspicious. To make matters worse, Nancy would cry and tremble whenever her swaddling was removed. Mother fell sick during the confinement month. Grandmother was afraid, so she advised Father to give Nancy away.

It was not easy to get someone to adopt Nancy given the inauspicious time and year she was born. So Father and Grandmother took Nancy to the orphanage. It must have been hard on Father. But he never talked to any of his children about Nancy. Mother, on the other hand, would relate this to the neighbors during their chitchat. She said Nancy cried and trembled because I pulled the pillow on which she was lying. I was selfish! Somehow, whatever I did, even as a one-year-old baby, seemed wrong.

For many years Mother talked about Nancy. But there was no attempt to locate and reunite with her. I was too ignorant to do anything until much later when I completed my schooling. It then dawned on me to write to the orphanage, and I did just that. The reply came after several weeks: Nancy passed away three months after she was given to the orphanage. When I relayed the news to Mother, there wasn't much reaction. Another child she was not close to.

I would be most curious whenever someone mentioned seeing another girl or woman resembling me. But I have yet to meet someone who looks so like me!

Mother delivered Betty and Annie in the cabin. In both instances, Father engaged a midwife. During those days, having a midwife to deliver a baby was common. I suppose it was more convenient than going to the hospital.

They were disappointed with having girls again. Mother wanted to give Betty away, but Grandmother offered to take care of Betty. So Betty was brought up by Grandmother until she was ready to attend school.

Mother gave Annie to First-Uncle upon Grandmother's advice. The woman with whom First-Uncle lived was unable to conceive.

First-Uncle was always gambling. Grandmother hoped that with a complete family, First-Uncle would change.

At first, First-Uncle's mate doted on Annie. But when Annie was one year old, she left First-Uncle. So Annie also ended up with Grandmother. She never came home to live with us. Neither did she return to First-Uncle. He remained unattached for the rest of life, gambling away all his earnings. In fact he had a few brushes with the law. On one occasion, he was accused of being a member of a secret society, just because he had a tattoo on his body. The family had to engage a lawyer to defend him. That incident had Mother all over the place and appearing in court to see and hear what was happening. And she had lots to relay to her siblings, imitating the way the lawyer spoke, too.

My parents were obsessed with having a male child. But each delivery was a disappointment. Father wanted a son to carry his family name and worship his ancestors when he passed on.

So they were delighted when Heng was born—ten years after me. Now, they had a son! It was on a memorable day for all of Singapore, too—May 30, 1959, the day we gained self-government. There was great celebration.

Father had never been able to give any of us girls a proper Chinese name. For one thing, he could not write Chinese. English names came easily to his mind. But for Heng, it was different. Heng was named after the Member of Parliament in our constituency. He had the same surname, too.

Friends and neighbors offered gifts like biscuits, eggs, and chicken essence for Mother. Some friends even gave live chickens.

At the end of the first month, Mother cooked brown glutinous rice and red eggs[31] to distribute with ang ku kueh to friends and relatives. More gifts came in, this time for

---

[31] Signifying happiness

Heng—pieces of cloth with striped patterns for Mother to sew for his clothes.

All the sisters doted on Heng. He was our first brother. But Heng gradually became the subject of much quarreling between Mother and Father—and Mother and the rest of us. Mother was too protective of Heng. She often chided us for innocent acts that she deemed hurting or insulting to her son.

Not long after Heng was born, Mother had a miscarriage. Her water bag burst outside a neighbor's room. She told me to clean up the place. I was puzzled at how Mother could spill so much water. After she went to the hospital, I overheard Father tell a neighbor that Mother lost a pair of twins. Later Mother said both were boys.

It was a great blow for Father. But Father never showed his feelings. I often wondered what it would have been like if the twin boys had survived. Maybe life for the rest of us children would have been much different.

Chapter 10

Late for Schooling

We had lived in that cabin for three years, and it was about time for me to attend school. During that period, schooling was not compulsory.

One day Father took me to a school in a convent. The nuns looked formidable. I was quite alarmed. I could not understand what they were talking about. I think I was accepted because Father bought a textbook to prepare me for school.

Once home, Father tried to teach me to read.

"I am Old Lob," he said.

"I am Old Lob," I repeated after him.

Then he pointed at the words. I could not remember which was which. Whatever he tried, I just could not remember. Thinking I was being stubborn, he took out the cane. But I still could not remember. Frustrated, he threw down the cane, and from that day, he never tried to make me read again.

Father had schooling until Primary Four. He could read English, but he lacked the ability to teach. It was really frustrating for him to see me looking so blank.

Before I could attend that school in the convent, Father was transferred to work in a ward at the General Hospital. So we moved to a different house again. General Hospital was too far from Oukang. It was impossible for me to travel to school daily. My schooling had to wait.

This delay had a huge impact on my life and possibly my early development. I joined a cohort of students that was much impacted by major changes in Singapore's history in later years.

In our next home, my parents could not get me a place in the English school nearby. But there were two Chinese schools. Father simply refused to register me in a Chinese school. He saw no future in a Chinese education. Also, in those days, Chinese schools were run privately. It was hard for Father to pay the school fees.

Father was also adamant that I become a clerk. In his workplace, all clerks were superior to him. They had better pay and better work lives. So he wanted me to have an English education and become a clerk. He always wanted the best for me!

Well, it must have dawned on Father that I was going to lose out to my peers. So he collected used record books—those discarded by the hospital administration—and tore off the used pages, leaving the few blank ones. Then he used a ruler and pencil to draw big squares and filled the top rows with A, B, C...; 1, 2, 3...; and so on for me to copy.

I struggled to form the characters. Both parents laughed over my squiggles. They found it amusing and showed my "artwork" to the neighbors.

For many years, one such record book sat on our dressing table supporting an electric fan. Every now and then, my parents would pull it out to show friends and relatives—like a big joke!

About a year later, I was finally admitted to the English primary school down the road. Father was excited. He bought me a brown school bag with a hard casing. It looked like a suitcase and was commonly carried in those days. Then he painted my name in white paint on it, with big, bold capital letters for one and all to see, except me. I could not read at all!

Several days into school, I heard boys calling me at every turn of the corridor.

"Why did you do that?" I demanded of my father

"So that you will not lose your bag," he said, laughing.

I was mad, so he brushed another coat of dark paint over my name. But the outlines still showed.

On the day before school, Mother took me to a temple to make offerings to Confucius. She offered a cooked chicken with its heart stuck in the beak. After that she made me eat the chicken heart, saying I would have a heart for learning.

Why couldn't she give me something to eat so that I could "have a heart" for her?

In any case, for many years Mother kept up this practice. Just before school reopened in a brand-new year, I would have to pray to Confucius and eat a chicken heart.

On my first day at school, Father took me there and left me in the classroom. Everyone was a stranger to me. I felt very lonely.

The class teacher called out our names. Parents and their charges went to her. I waited, but I was not called.

It was recess time when Mother finally came. The other children had vacated the classroom.

"Did the teacher call you?" Mother asked. I shook my head. The teacher had just finished her registration of the last child. Mother approached her.

"Lee Tian Sang?" the teacher asked Mother.

"That's the father's name." Mother said in Hokkien. "She is Lee Dee Dee."

"You are Lily Lee?" the teacher asked me in English. I stared at her blankly.

How was I to know I was Lily Lee? They all called me Ali. Till then, I only knew I was

Ali. And this teacher simply refused to speak Hokkien to me when she could speak to Mother. I was feeling miserable. The future looked bleak!

Chapter 11

Life in the Hospital Quarters

My third home was in a long, three-story building built to house families of hospital staff. It was close to the hospital grounds, along a road protected by a gate, with a narrow opening for pedestrians and cyclists. No cars or buses could enter. The gate would be opened only during emergencies to allow police cars and ambulances to enter. Often when Grandmother paid a visit, she would tell the taxi driver to bring her to Siao Lang Keng Kak.[32] She would alight on the road that ran

---

[32] Hokkien term meaning the corner of a mental institution—it seemed previously there was a mental hospital in this area.

alongside ours, and enter the area through an opening in the wall separating the two roads.

Each family in the building occupied a large room along a common corridor that ran through the length of the building. Across the corridor and directly opposite each room were a small kitchen, a wash area, and just enough space for a small dining table and chairs.

There were four common staircases, each comparatively much wider than those in private apartments. They were situated on each end of the building, and the other two were spaced out in the middle. On each floor, the staircase led to a big square spanning across the corridor. Right across from the square, another corridor, perpendicular to the first, led to two common toilets, one for males and the other for females. This corridor was divided lengthwise in the middle by a wall.

There was only one big bathroom and five waste cubicles in each toilet. Occupants in these quarters had to take turns bathing.

Some of them would bathe together. They would draw water from a huge bathtub. The bathtub was made of bricks laid to form a rectangle with one corner of the bathroom. Sometimes naughty children climbed in and had a good swim. Of course, the neighbors would be screaming mad when they found out. Hence, quarrels often arose over the use of the bathroom.

The cubicles were often unclean because of faulty cisterns or people not doing their business properly. We often had to maneuver our way around the "gold nuggets" to get to the bathroom and cubicles. The place looked pretty alarming during evenings when the lights were not turned on and in the morning when the lights went off too early. There were many occasions when there was a blackout and we had to use candlelight to find our way there.

There had been incidents of Peeping Toms— men or boys hiding in the cubicle next to the bathroom to look through a gap between the wall and the ceiling. When the woman inside happened to look up and saw a face, she would scream and the neighbors would come running. By then, the Peeping Tom had bolted.

Yet, throughout our stay in this place, neither parent ever warned us of possible danger lurking in the common toilets. They avoided all talks about sexuality. In school there was no sex education either. So I knew next to nothing about how babies were made— or ever thought of the possibility of getting raped in those cubicles. We were just simply forbidden to leave the room in the evenings to answer nature's call.

Life here was a far cry from the solitude in the cabin. Neighbors could see each other doing their household chores. In the morning there were cheery greetings: "早安,"[33] "selamat pagi,"[34] or in whatever language or dialect they spoke. Neighbors talked to one another and helped each other. The pace was much slower.

---

[33] Good morning in Chinese.
[34] Good morning in Malay.

But living so close to each other, neighbors often quarreled. Sometimes it got so bad the hospital administration had to intervene.

We often received food from the neighbors living immediately around us. It was in this place that I learned there were so many colored people, so many languages, and so many cuisines. It was a hodgepodge of religion and culture, too.

But Mother hated noise. Unless we were doing housework, she forbade us from spending much time outside the room. We were told not to go to the neighbors' rooms to chitchat. Whenever a neighbor came over to talk to us, she would get upset.

So, although it was a great place to immerse ourselves in the multicultural lives of Singapore, most of my time was spent within the four walls of the room.

Mother insisted on keeping everything in our living quarters clean. The neighbors often said,

"Ah Sang Soh is very clean." She swelled with pride and insisted we children keep clean, too.

Cleanliness was Mother's hallmark! She had to maintain her reputation. From very young, we children had to clean the house, and wash clothes and utensils.

Every morning, I swept the room and wiped the floor. Mother wanted the corridor area outside our room washed as well. But food vendors and neighbors going to work or school traversed the corridor. Often dirty footprints appeared on the wet, newly cleaned floor. It was frustrating. But Mother insisted the washing must be done in the morning, and there was no bargaining!

In the late afternoon, before dinnertime, the floor had to be swept again. Otherwise, I got another earful.

Housework also took priority over schoolwork. Mother never checked whether we did our school assignments. She only insisted on housework done on time.

Outside our room, food vendors plied their wares along the corridors, balancing poles on their shoulders. Pots and baskets hung from both ends of their poles. They sold yong tau foo,[35] soon kueh,[36] ang ku kueh, putu mayam,[37] and mee siam.[38] These hawker wares of Chinese, Indian, or Malay origin were often made from rice. They sold for as little as five cents apiece or ten cents a bowl. After eating, we could still ask for a refill of the soup.

Sometimes, the Indian man came with a big basket perched on his turban. His hard, crusty bread made in the shape of a gun was so fragrant—just yummy!

The candy man came occasionally making his soft, white, sticky candy on a tray. He danced

---

[35] Chinese soup dish of tofu, ladies' fingers (okra), and eggplants stuffed with fish paste.

[36] Steamed rice dumpling stuffed with turnips and bamboo shoots.

[37] Steamed rice noodle shaped in the form of a net, eaten with ground fresh coconut and brown sugar.

[38] Spicy rice noodle with gravy, served with chili paste and lime juice.

and sang like a madman. Mother kept us away from him.

In those days, the hawker scene was really colorful and the cuisine so much more authentic and personal. Unfortunately, my family was making ends meet. Most often, I saw the vendors whisk past our room.

Along the part of the corridor where I lived, there were three other girls.

Cindy was three years older than me. She lived with her mother, aged grandmother, and an elder brother in the corner room to our right, just beside the common staircase. Both Cindy and her brother went to a Chinese school. Her sailor father came home once in a long, long while. But every time his homestay would end with an acrimonious quarrel with Cindy's mother.

Kathy lived three rooms away to my left, just before the corridor led to a small flight of steps down to another section of the building. She went to an English school. Her single mother worked at the General Hospital. Her elder brother and sister-in-law lived with them.

Sally lived in the next room to my left. She also went to an English school. Her mother, Chui Lian, was also single and working at the General Hospital. Sally had an elder brother. Her elderly grandmother lived in an attap[39] hut nearby.

Kathy and Sally were the same age and two years ahead of me in school.

I am not sure how Kathy and Sally's mothers lost their spouses—poor relationship or were the men killed during the Japanese occupation? Nevertheless, Kathy and Sally were often left to their own devices as their mothers worked shifts in the wards.

With Mother's restraining, I was never really able to form intimate friendships with these girls.

---

[39] The wattle and leaves of a palm tree

Of the three I liked Cindy most. She was a cheerful girl and the first person I saw writing Chinese characters with a brush and black ink. She had lots of school assignments of this sort. When not working on her assignments, she would be doing housework or selling ice cream in a portable thermal can. In those days the ice cream was made from starch. A big drum filled with ice and salt was used to freeze the ice cream onto a stick.

It was the first time I heard Hockchew[40] spoken. Cindy's grandmother was often calling for her. "Se Yu, Se Yu!"

"Cho xie nor?" Cindy would reply. It took me some time to figure out that "Cho xie nor?" means "What do you want?"

Well, not long after we moved there, Cindy's grandmother suddenly became very ill. She was gasping for breath on her deathbed. Mother went over to their room and they were

---

[40] Another Chinese dialect

all crying and calling her name. But she passed away.

That was also the first time I experienced a funeral wake. Neighbors helped with the preparation of meals and served drinks to the guests. Groundnuts and melon seeds were offered to the guests, too. Everyone seemed to be at the wake and pretty busy. The gotong royong[41] spirit, as the Malays called it, was very much alive in this community. Whenever someone needed help, neighbors would rally around. In times of crises, this support was very comforting indeed. So it pained me to see this disappearing in modern Singapore.

For whatever reason, Cindy stopped schooling very early. Her mother had her match made to a Malaysian across the causeway. His family was well to do. I believe Cindy agreed quite mindlessly to this match, and the marriage did not last. She eventually came home to her

---

[41] Spirit of neighbors rallying round whenever assistance is required

mother and worked as a cleaner to raise her one and only daughter.

On the other hand, Kathy and Sally were more playful. On festive occasions, they joined the neighbors in the gambling. I often wondered where they got so much money. I simply had none at all to spare. All the money in the ang pows I received from relatives during Chinese New Year were surrendered to Mother.

Sally also loved to switch on the Redifusion loud, blaring out Elvis Presley and Cliff Richard's songs. And she would sing along with them— her favorite: "Judy, Judy, Judy."

Both Kathy and Sally played hard on school days and failed their school examinations most of the time. During their final GCE[42] "O" Level Exams period, both sat outside their rooms into the wee hours, trying to cram as

---

[42] General Certificate of Education from Cambridge University, UK

much into their heads as possible. They failed nevertheless.

But both girls found boyfriends immediately after the exams and got married. As far as I know, they raised children and were well supported by their husbands throughout their lives.

The lesson learned: it doesn't seem beneficial to be a goody-goody. I used to envy Kathy and Sally. They did not do well in school and did not work hard. Yet they were rewarded with much better lives than Cindy.

Chapter 12

Blame, Shame, and Care

In a place that was so public, every commotion in a room would send the neighbors running to the door. When Mother got upset, she took out her cane, and the shouting and screaming would draw a crowd.

Neighbors would try to restrain her and coax us children to ask for forgiveness. "Say you will never do that again."

No way, no way. I refused to say that.

Afterward Mother would say, "See, it is so shameful. All the neighbors can see the cane marks. It was all due to your doing. Shows how bad you are!"

It was better to be thrashed in the cabin than in this place! Mother seemed to revel in being a strict parent. Other people's children were not so well behaved. Hers were, all due to her good teaching.

On many occasions, the beating was not due to ill intention or wrongdoing on our part. Knowing our mother, each of us children was wrapped up in his or her own inner world, afraid to communicate thoughts and feelings. We hardly fought or quarreled. So, you might ask, how did that whipping come about?

I think when Mother got upset, she had to let out all her negative energy. And she did not know how to do that in other ways.

One day, there was leftover fabric from a beautiful piece of cloth used for Mother's samfoo. The friend who sewed the samfoo decided to make me a dress with it. I was thrilled. After washing, my dress became crumbled. I was ironing some other clothes, so enthusiastically I proceeded to iron my dress.

I was horrified to see the material curl and tear under the hot iron. Mother was furious when she saw what happened. She gave me a violent beating.

On another occasion, it was my school's sports day. The weather was hot and humid as I wandered aimlessly all over the big field. Everyone else watched the competitions. I had absolutely no interest in sports and did not know what to do. Finally I reached home drenched with perspiration. When Mother saw me in that sorry and dirty state, she beat me soundly. Next day, she refused to let me wear my uniform to school. Instead, I had to go in my home clothes.

I cried uncontrollably when the form teacher asked what happened. The whole class laughed. I was in Primary Two then. Children at that age probably knew nothing about empathy. They laughed quite unkindly when they saw something funny. For me, the sufferer, it was real pain and humiliation!

There was only one occasion when Mother found us siblings arguing. That was after Betty had returned home and started schooling. I caught Betty copying answers for her arithmetic assignment. When I told her that was not right, she became upset and started to cry. Without even asking what the matter was, Mother took out her cane and whipped both of us soundly. After that I never pried into my siblings' school assignments again.

Such discipline had not taught us much about right and wrong. My siblings avoided doing anything out of our normal activities. Rosie and Betty would religiously do all the housework, complete their school assignments early—whether correctly or otherwise—and go to bed early. By eight o'clock, they would all be sleeping.

As for me, with each beating, I felt more and more that such punishment was unjust.

Beatings aside, Mother did her best to provide for us children in her own way.

She wanted a sewing machine to sew for the family. So she saved to buy one with a leg paddle. Then she made clothes for Rosie and me. She would sew two similar pieces. When she took us out for visits, Rosie and I would be similarly dressed. Friends and relatives commented on her fine workmanship.

But Rosie and I hated to be identical. "Don't sew the same pattern please," I would plead.

I was dying to try my hands on the sewing machine, too. But my feet could not reach the paddle. When I grew big enough, I took over the sewing. I would let Mother sew Rosie's piece first. Then, when she used the border with the floral design on the top front, I would use the plain part for the top and leave the floral border at the bottom of the skirt so I looked different!

"Don't you look like me!" I told Rosie.

"Don't you look like me!" she returned.

For years Rosie and I strived to look different. Rosie refused to wear clothes I had worn. I was bigger than her, so I did not take hand-me-downs from her.

Rosie was a beauty with big eyes and rosy, puffy cheeks. Neighbors who saw her for the first time would gasp and comment on her beauty. Some even pinched her cheeks.

But nobody took a second look at me. My eyes were too small, and I was scrawny.

Poor as we were, we seldom had hand-me-downs or used things from others. Father always made sure we had new dresses and shoes for Chinese New Year. But the dresses were often oversized. School uniforms were oversized, too. Once, a classmate announced, "Lily wears cheongsam."[43] I burned with shame!

---

[43] Cantonese term for a shapely long dress with Mandarin collar

Mother's bed was raised with bricks so she could store our belongings underneath it. It was placed under the window in one corner of the room.

One particular fateful day, Father had parked his wooden deck chair right beside the bed.

Mother looked out of the window and exclaimed, "There are policemen downstairs!"

Excitedly, I climbed onto the bed and looked out of the window. Then, seeing nothing of real interest, I took a jump for the floor. My face hit the top wooden corner of the deck chair. I screamed with pain. Mother and neighbors came rushing. Mother grabbed hold of me and rubbed my right cheek vigorously. It was so painful! I struggled hard to break away from her grip, but I was held down. Everyone was sure I was going to be disfigured!

For days Mother agonized over my swollen, blue-black cheek. She rubbed it with hot water.

Then, still feeling unsure, she rubbed hot hard-boiled eggs over it. Finally she gave up.

Eventually, the swelling subsided and I looked normal—until I smiled. Hey, I got a dimple!

Those were the days when home remedies abounded. We were so poor that it never occurred to anyone I might need medical attention.

When Rosie had mumps, Mother brushed her jaws with a bluish liquid. She said Rosie had the skin of a pig's head, so she needed to ward off the tiger. As if tigers could suddenly appear out of nowhere!

As far as I can remember, my two front teeth were missing. Mother said it was the result of too many sweets. First-Uncle called me "Boh Geh"—toothless! And I seemed to have countless toothaches.

Once I was anesthetized while a tooth was extracted. I was alarmed when a hospital staff member placed a rubber cup over my mouth. I felt horrible when I regained consciousness.

On another occasion, Father waited with me at the dental clinic in the General Hospital. The hospital setting with its antiseptic smell and the long wait simply built up the tension in me. When they finally put me in the dental chair, I screamed and refused to have my tooth extracted. The nurses scolded Father and told us to leave.

Father was gentle. He did not push the issue as he walked home with me, wheeling his bicycle.

But Mother would not let the matter rest. She had her own dental appointment in Chinatown. Rosie and I played while she was attended to in a separate room.

When she was done, Mother told the dentist my problem. The dentist agreed to extract my tooth. Together with his assistant, they caught hold of me and forcibly did the job. I screamed and struggled throughout the whole treatment. But the job was done.

That incident left a mark. In later years I would wait until the pain was most unbearable before I would visit the dentist.

Chapter 13

My Early Days in School

The first few days at school were horrible. I could only speak Hokkien. The teacher spoke English. She simply avoided talking in dialect. My classmates seemed to have been to kindergarten or taught by older siblings. So it looked like they were better than me. The world there was strange to a girl who had spent most of her time in a room.

At recess, everyone jostled in the tuck shop for food. Some had parents buying for them, but I was alone. So I ended up eating sweets and kachang puteh[44]—best not to carry hot food or soup to spill.

---

[44] Malay word for an assortment of nuts

In this strange world, the hours seemed to drag. I felt tense and sometimes my stomach churned with gas. Gradually, I settled into a routine, walking to and from school alone.

For a child used to the confines of a room, the open world with lots of strange people was really frightening. I felt more alone in that crowd.

However, I was by nature talkative. Soon I started talking to the children around me. Sometimes the teacher would say, "Lily, stop talking and stand up!"

When the class got really rowdy, everyone was punished with standing. The teacher would gradually ask a few well-behaved students to sit down. But not me, I stood with the rest. Sometimes we were asked to stand on the chairs or even on the desks!

How could I ever expect a teacher to like me? I was a child from the slums, uncouth and doomed for failure!

One day, the teacher was making sounds with the alphabets. She was showing how the sounds combined into words. It looked easy to pronounce words once you grasped the sounds of the vowels and consonants. I really paid attention. Wow, I could read the words on my own!

That was when I developed an interest in reading. I read whatever children's books were available on the classroom bookshelves. Later on, when I could, I borrowed storybooks from the school library. Stories about little people called pixies intrigued me. I entered an imaginary world of fairies, animals, and adventure. Life was never dull when I settled into my dream world!

Seeing my interest, Father collected any children's books he could from the Red Cross library. These were old books and magazines given to inpatients to kill time. I would wake up in the night to answer to nature's call and find a book lying on the table. Next morning, it was gone.

"Where is the book?"

"What book?" Father feigned ignorance.

Reading became my most pleasurable pass time. When the storybooks ran out, I read textbooks. My grades improved. I became one of the top students in my class.

And now Mother started to brag about how clever her eldest daughter was. She could go on ad nauseam until her siblings groaned.

My young aunties threw up their arms in despair. How could they compare with Ali? But Grandmother had the answer. "You can't beat Ali. She did all the learning before she was born." As if I stored all the knowledge in my stomach before I came into this world!

For me, it was not about getting grades to please Mother or Father. I just simply enjoyed learning.

While reading gave me pleasure, mathematics was my forte. In school I religiously counted ice-cream sticks and obediently did all the arithmetic assigned. Gradually I could do the sums mentally. I just loved arithmetic.

When Father came across me doing my sums, he showed me more advanced ways of doing addition. I grasped the concepts immediately. He was thrilled and gave me more problems to solve. Gradually I whisked beyond Father's realm into my own world of problem solving.

Father's teachings always came in small doses. But they were more fun, and we both enjoyed my learning.

But I hated physical education. I could not run fast. I always came in last in a race. And whenever there was a competitive sport, the other students didn't want me on their teams. Because of this, I was often lonely during recess. My classmates found me a handicap in their games. They would rather not ask me at all.

Rosie entered the same school a year after me. Although a crybaby, she was very well behaved. There was never a complaint from her teachers throughout her school career. She faithfully did her work and handed in her assignments on time. Her grades were below average, but that did not bother the teachers.

Initially my parents grumbled about Rosie's performance. Eventually, however, they stopped; they could do nothing to help her.

Betty was much the same as Rosie. My parents never heard from the teachers. It never occurred to them to find out what was wrong with Rosie and Betty's studies. Simply put, they decided, both were not bright. But later in adult life, Rosie and Betty were the best workers in their offices. Sad thing was they had to do lots of catching up in skill and knowledge to make up for lost time.

After Rosie entered the same school, we often walked home together. In those days, when every school had morning and afternoon sessions, both of us were placed in the same sessions. Between school and home was one straight road. Along the way, a hawker pushed a cart selling drinks and tidbits. For five cents, we could get two cups of drinks. We would save money from recess and buy two cups— pineapple or even lychee drinks.

Enterprising Malay neighbors put up stalls to sell goreng pisang,[45] kledek,[46] and other finger food. But more often than not, we could only afford drinks.

The teachers did get to like me after all. I was always responsive in class, prepared for the next lesson, and ready to take up any challenging task—except when it came to sports.

During my final year in the primary school, everyone was thinking about which secondary school they would like to attend. But I had no idea at all. My life was so confined that I really

---

[45] Deep-fried bananas
[46] Deep-fried tapioca

did not know much about the world beyond home and school.

One day, my form teacher, Mrs. Bartholomew, took me aside.

"Have you any idea which school to choose after the entrance examination?"

"I don't know."

"You stand a good chance to get into a top school. But don't choose an aided school. These schools expect donations from parents, and most of the parents there can afford tuition. If you have no tuition, you might lose out to your other schoolmates. I think you should be able to get into top government schools like Raffles' Girls or Crescent Girls. I suggest you choose these two."

When the application papers came, I made Raffles' Girls Secondary School (RGS) my first choice, and I was given a place in RGS. Father was elated. But Mother said, "So far away, I think you should change school."

For Mother, anywhere beyond walking distance from home was far. And to me, RGS was indeed a strange and far-off destination.

Luckily, Mother did not ask for a change of school. I would have been a laughingstock. That year, RGS had only three classes for new students. In the year before there were thirteen classes, while in the year after there were eleven. So it was really not easy to secure a place in RGS. I was lucky.

Chapter 14

The Strange World Beyond Home

For someone like me, RGS seemed really far from home. My parents arranged for Uncle Ong to take me there and back. Uncle Ong made a living by ferrying children to and from schools. This was against the law, but many men like him operated pirate taxis to earn their daily bread. He charged a monthly fee of ten dollars.

Every school day at noon, I would wait at the bus stop just outside my primary school. By the time Uncle Ong picked me up, the car was quite full of RGS girls. There were about five or six of us. Except for one who took the front seat, the rest squeezed into the back. We always exceeded the legal seating capacity. So whenever we saw the traffic police, Uncle Ong would ask some of us to duck our heads down.

School dismissed around six o'clock in the evening. We waited outside RGS's main gate for Uncle Ong. Most times he would appear after six thirty. His business was good, so we had no choice but to wait our turn.

By the time I reached home, it would be quite dark. The rest of the family would have eaten their dinner. Mother expected me to eat dinner and clean up all the pots and pans.

A Cantonese serial drama on Redifusion started at seven-thirty in the evening. That was the favorite pastime I shared with Mother and my sisters. I would rush through my routine so I could settle down to immerse myself in the drama. Incidentally, that was how I picked up smatterings of the Cantonese dialect.

In the initial days at RGS, adjusting to changes was quite daunting. The waiting for transport and the darkness of the evenings often gave me a sense of foreboding.

As an institution, RGS was not exactly friendly. The teachers came into the class, taught their subjects, and left. They paid no attention to students' needs. Focus was on sports and extracurricular activities. Every time the same few popular and vocal students were voted into offices.

Many RGS girls had parents who were alumni of the school or Raffles Institution, the brother school of RGS. Having parents who were professional made a big difference. The girls seemed so sure of themselves. They formed cliques. Poor ones like me were often left out of their socializing.

The school placed great importance on sports. So, each of us was assigned to one of five houses named after past principals of the school. While the school sessions for the lower secondary students were in the afternoon, house practices were held in the morning, one specific morning a week for each of the houses.

With his heavy load of regular students, Uncle Ong could not go out of his way to fetch me for house practice. So I had to go to school by public transport.

There was only one bus service from the nearest bus stop—the one outside my primary school. In those days, the buses were crowded during peak hours. One had to literally squeeze in and cling to the railings. Some people stood on the steps of the opened door as the bus moved. Somewhere near Great World, I changed to another bus service that took me to RGS. Jostling with the crowd and changing buses was an alarming experience.

The first time, the experience was really awful. Finding my way, waiting anxiously for the buses, and squeezing into them, built up tension inside me. I was close to tears when I finally arrived.

The house practices—running, jumping, and throwing javelins and discuses—to determine the best representatives for the house simply bored me to death! I wished to be excused from all of them.

The lack of exposure to the outside world certainly took its toll on me. The world seemed so strange and unfriendly. Suddenly I was confronted with an onslaught of demands. The adjustment to secondary school life was painful and took quite some time. Nevertheless, overcome I did—painful but necessary.

My classmates were very studious. There was this air of competition that worried me. I missed the easy days in the primary school when we played and only quarreled over who should get less marks after the exams—so I could be first in class!

The teachers at RGS were also much less encouraging. For example, it was impossible to complete our art pieces within two periods of lesson time. So, most of us took our assignments home to complete over the weekends—only to get one mark out of ten for our hard work. And we received no suggestions to make our pieces better.

I cannot recollect learning any specific skills that allowed me to be a better artist or learner. Some classmates were reciting whole chunks of information from their notes or textbooks. They were the cream of the crop in their primary schools and eager to do well in RGS, too. But memorizing chunks of texts did not go down well with me at all.

That was the time when I started to feel self-conscious. I was afraid to approach any teacher for assistance. And none ever came to me to inquire why I did not do well or why I did better.

As for classmates, those who had more resources appeared to stick together. Those, like me, who came from humbler families, looked even more anxious whenever someone mentioned something that seemed strange—not in their textbooks. Tension was especially high during exam periods.

I became shy and avoided crowded places. I used to go down the slope at the end of the road to run errands for Mother, but now I would try to get Rosie to do them.

About that time Singapore started its first television broadcasting station. Black-and-white television sets came onto the scene, but we were too poor to buy one. So my brother Heng would gather with other children outside a neighbor's room to watch the shows. At mealtime, Rosie would shout for him to come home. Down the corridor, all the neighbors could hear her voice. I just went about my own affairs and never joined them at their television sets.

As this was a multiracial place, Heng played with Malay and Indian children. Often they quarreled and Rosie had to intervene. She would scold those children when she felt they were in the wrong. In one instance, an Indian boy complained about Heng using a vulgar Indian word on him. But Heng said the boy used that word first. Not knowing what it meant, he imitated the boy. Wow, Rosie really gave the boy an earful!

Neighbors often compared Rosie and me to Mother. We were so different, they said. Rosie was noisy, and I was simply quiet.

It was a really painful period for me. I couldn't understand myself. Why was I so afraid of meeting people? And it was worse if the other party was of the opposite gender. So I just absorbed myself in my books.

Mother's menstrual cycle seemed to play havoc again. She complained of heavy menstruation and went to the hospital often. Finally the doctors recommended a hysterectomy. Mother was hospitalized for a week, leaving the family to our own devices.

Being the eldest child in the family, I took charge of the cooking. In those days, we did not own a fridge so we had to buy fresh food daily. But I was afraid to go to the marketplace. Thus I specified what to buy, and Rosie went with my instructions. I would make sure not to spend more than a dollar and fifty cents for our family's three meals. Rosie faithfully did as told, and I struggled through the cooking. Father never complained. He just let us be.

We were frugal. It never occurred to me to cook anything special beyond the three basic meals. Compared to Mother, the food I cooked was bland, but my siblings neither complained nor refused to eat.

When Mother came home from the hospital, I was busy washing up pots and pans. While Rosie and the others went to welcome her, I continued with the housework. Mother was not pleased. She said I was indifferent about her condition. I had "no heart" for her.

Subconsciously, yes, maybe I had no love for Mother. Her frequent accusations did not help at all. I was just tired of hearing them.

When I turned twelve years old, Mother decided she could not beat me anymore. But the emotional abuse that followed was much more painful than the physical abuse.

Chapter 15

Poverty

Our wash area overlooked a backyard where wild plants and trees grew randomly. Farther away, up a slope, there were some attap huts. People living there reared chickens and ducks. Often the ducks came close to lay eggs on the grass.

In the morning, as he brushed his teeth at the wash area, Father could spot the newly laid eggs. He would toss out his tin mug, go into the room, and give sleeping Rosie a light kick. That was the cue! Rosie would get up and run down the stairs into the backyard to look for the tin mug and the eggs.

Was it greed? Well, the whole family relied on Father's income. Every cent counted. We seldom had treats. When he could, Father would bring home an orange, banana, or any fruit that patients in the ward left uneaten during mealtime.

Once a year during Christmas, his supervisor would give him a gift. If it was chocolate, that was a real treat for us! Most of the time, however, it was just a bath towel.

Down the corridor, every family had a tin in their wash area to hold leftovers from their meal. In the evening, a woman would come by with a big pail. She emptied all the contents from the tins into her pail to feed the pigs she reared in a farm nearby. (Those were the days in Singapore when pigs roamed about. In some places there was a constant stench from their dung.) For all our contributions to the pigs, the woman would give each family ten hen eggs on Chinese New Year's Eve. That was a real bonus, too!

It was a good recycling arrangement. My family certainly could do with the extra ten eggs. And nobody complained about hygiene.

The family was growing, and expenses were increasing, but Father's income was not. For a long time Mother was toying with the idea of joining the workforce. So, when she received news that the General Hospital was recruiting attendants, Mother applied along with Kathy's sister-in-law. They went for the interview, but Mother was rejected.

Then Mother worked as a housemaid to a foreign family. After two days, her menstruation became heavy, and she stopped working.

Eventually Mother hit on an idea. She had seen Grandfather loan money to his colleagues and charge interest for it. In this poor neighborhood, people were often urgently in need of cash. So Mother borrowed some money from Grandfather and started her own money-lending business. Slowly we saw better food on the table.

Logically, when there is less worry about money, life should be more peaceful. For a short while it was.

But eventually, the sense of power got into Mother's head. Her voice grew louder. She became more dissatisfied with Father. Often, she would complain about how much she had done for the family and how useless Father was. Sometimes, she even accused Father of stealing her money.

I am not sure why. Was it because I was the eldest child? Mother's complaints and nagging were often directed at me, and they got on my nerves. I cried and promised to pay back every cent Father owed her. But that seemed to incense her even more.

I had crying spells and went to school crying uncontrollably. My classmates were puzzled, but none asked me why. Even if they had, I could not articulate my feelings.

At night, the dreams were horrible. I dreamed of losing my way and hurrying through strange places. Sometimes I saw dead bodies. On some occasions, I dreamed that Mother told me she was going to die, and I woke up to find my eyes all wet.

Sometimes, out of the blue, I started to gasp for breath and wanted to throw up, too. It was horrifying. When the spells passed, I felt so weak.

Mother was alarmed. She would rub eucalyptus oil over my forehead and give me a hot drink. But when the spells passed, she would make a joke of my condition. Other family members likewise thought this was just an idiosyncrasy on my part.

Like the panic attacks, the migraines came suddenly. My vision would become blurred. I foamed at the mouth and one side of my head throbbed. The headaches usually lasted about a day. Then I felt odd for a few more days.

But the worst was the urine. I had dreams about getting on a toilet to answer nature's call—and I actually let go. The feeling of urine wetting my blanket and bedding filled me with shame. In the morning, Mother would give me a sound scolding and even jeered at me. The other siblings, not comprehending, just joked about it.

It never occurred to anyone that I needed help. I was miserable and felt ashamed of myself. And my family's jeering and teasing made it worse. So I never confided in anyone.

Chapter 16

Mother and Her Insecurities

Not long after her hysterectomy, Mother started to complain about pain all over her body. She visited many doctors, but they could not tell her what was wrong. Frequently she had headaches and gastric pain. She would douse herself with eucalyptus oil, and the whole room smelled of it.

When Mother got sick, the atmosphere at home became very gloomy. We dared not laugh or be lighthearted in case she accused us of being heartless.

The sicker Mother was, the more protective she became of Heng. She would jump at us for chiding him or find faults with remarks we made to him or about him. And she got anxious very easily.

Even at that tender age, I often suspected Mother's illness was more psychological than physical. The operation seemed to make her worse. Her anxiety took a heavy grip on all of us. Life became even more miserable.

To make matters worse, that was a period of uncertainty for Singapore. It was 1964. Singapore had just merged with Malaya to form Malaysia. There were often talks about the need to promote racial harmony. Unlike some other parts of Singapore, in the area where my family lived different races mingled and worked together. As a child who was very ignorant, all these issues of the country meant nothing to me. If the school asked me to sing "God Saves the Queen," I would do just that. At that time, we were singing "Negara Ku,"[47] so it was most alarming when racial fights happened at our doorsteps.

---

[47] Malaysia's national anthem

From my window I could see a mosque. It stood beside an opening on the other side of the wall that ran along the road. Rumors were rife that the Malays kept parangs[48] in the mosque. Sally's mother, Chui Lian, often relayed rumors to Mother. Mother became quite apprehensive and insisted we stay in the room when there was nothing to do outside.

At the dead end of the road and below the slope was a Chinese community where gangsters abounded. Chinese youths formed the gangs and could be pretty violent when provoked. So gang fights were common.

One night, in July 1964, there was news that riots had broken out in Geylang.[49] I was not sure how that triggered those gangsters to fight. They attacked the Malays, threw glass bottles, and wielded knives, too. Inevitably

---

[48] Long knives
[49] An area in Singapore where the residents were mostly Malays

there were casualties. Chui Lian relayed a description of a person bleeding to death.

The atmosphere became tense. Next day, neighbors gathered to discuss what to do. They decided to keep a vigil and deploy all women and children to a safe place. Mother wanted to go with her children. I refused to join her; I wanted to be by Father's side. In the end, she decided not to leave.

That night, we sat tight in our locked room while the battle raged beneath our windows. We could hear shouting and screaming and the crashing of glass bottles. It was frightening!

Next morning the elders of both communities came together to talk. Each side agreed to restrain their youths. Luckily, they did. So an uneasy peace was restored.

I was never afraid of the other races. The occupants in these hospital quarters got along quite well. Although there were quarrels among neighbors, these were nonracial. During festive occasions, exchange of tidbits and food was common. So we were more wary of the youths coming from below the road than the other races.

This incident made Mother even more nervous. She got Father to make extra shutters for our windows and only door.

In those days, much of Singapore was in squatters. Attap huts and huts with corrugated aluminum roofs abounded. Incidents of fire were frequent, especially during Chinese New Year celebrations. The Chinese liked to play with firecrackers, lighting the wicks and throwing them high into the air. Sometimes these landed on attap roofs, triggering a fire.

The Bukit Ho Swee Fire in May 1961 destroyed twenty-two hundred homes and left sixteen thousand people homeless. This incident caused the Singapore government to look hard into permanent and public housing. Within a few years, housing estates sprung up. Everyone talked about owning his or her own flat—applying to the Housing and Development Board (HDB).

Mother was worried. Father would retire from work at age fifty-five. Then we would have to vacate our room and have nowhere to stay. She wanted an HDB flat, too.

She needed to apply for the flat but worried about eligibility. The family income was low. To boost that up, I had to join the workforce!

So, as HDB rolled out more flats and Mother's siblings moved into them, pressure for me to join the workforce also built up. Her constant argument was the waiting time. It took five or more years between application and being allocated a flat.

I was doing well enough in school. Everyone talked about going to the universities. I wanted to go, too. Getting there, however, might not be easy. But there were stories of students working part time and giving home tuition to support themselves. So I was hopeful. Throughout my school days, I received bursaries. The sums were small but still helpful. So I was confident I could receive financial aid from the government.

But Mother was adamant: no bursaries or scholarships! In those days, the Colombo Plan scholarships were the most prestigious. Only students with excellent grades were encouraged to apply. But the idea of me going abroad was too much for Mother. No, she forbade it! She had heard tales about children going abroad, never to return home again.

Then Grandfather became very sick. He had a severe stomachache and was in and out of the hospital. Everyone was concerned. Mother visited him often, and she confided in Chui Lian. Mother did not tell me anything about Grandfather's condition, so I gathered bits and pieces from her conversation with Chui Lian.

I remember the last time I saw Grandfather. He was sitting hunched over on the floor. He did not say much to me beyond the usual greetings.

But I saw a tear drop. By that age, there was no physical contact between him and me. I was awkward, not knowing how to console him. So we both kept a brave front and distance.

The illness lasted for quite a few months. Eventually Grandfather passed on.

When she received the news, Mother went off to help with the funeral preparation. I was instructed to sew mourning pants for everyone in my family. When I finally arrived at the wake, the coffin was closed, and I did not get a final glimpse of Grandfather.

Grandfather was my source of extra pocket money. Whatever he gave me, I would save to use for extra expenses like past examination papers. He passed on just when I started on the second (and last) year of my pre-university education. With his demise, I struggled even harder to optimize whatever savings I had left.

I broke down and cried profusely during the funeral. That evening, I heard crying voices around me when I was bathing alone in the public bathroom.

It was a hallucination, all right! The incident did not frighten me; however, I excused myself from attending the annual Qing Ming.[50] Much as I loved Grandfather, I could not bring myself to go near his grave site.

Grandfather was Mother's source of financial support. Knowing our financial situation, Grandfather would give my parents money every year to celebrate Chinese New Year. So, with his demise, Mother's sense of insecurity increased. She had to push me to work.

And now she had even more excuses. I had to contribute to the younger siblings' schooling. The actual situation was that Rosie and Betty were indifferent to studies. Heng had just started primary school, so it would be a long

---

[50] Around March and April everyone paid respects to their ancestors at the graveyards.

time before he needed financial support for his education. But because daughters did not belong to the family once they were married, it was futile to invest in their education. So Mother's excuses went on and on.

I was troubled by her reasoning. Panic attacks, migraines, and all my other idiosyncrasies occurred more frequently.

None of us knew how to handle Mother. Father distanced himself from it all. Life was miserable. Sometimes I hated Father for being a coward.

Chapter 17

First Boyfriend

I first met Harold in the chemistry department of the General Hospital. It was the long school vacation before we resumed studies in the following year. My school had arranged for me to spend a week there to learn how technicians worked.

Harold was from Raffles Institution (RI). He was not handsome at all and full of pimples, but I admired the long strides he took when he walked. He was shy, too. I believe I initiated the first conversation between us.

He was about my age and also preparing to take the GCE "O" Level Exams the following year. He dreamed of going on to tertiary education.

Besides academic studies, Harold was also active in extracurricular activities. He was the chief librarian for his school and a school prefect. And he seemed very confident.

I was not attracted to this boy at all. I had many crushes for older men but not for boys my age. Nevertheless, Harold became my source of support for the next three years of my life. To me, it was a platonic relationship.

Not long after we met, a little girl about ten years old appeared at my door. She carried a baby on her back. This girl gave me a handwritten note from Harold and went off.

I was surprised. I did not give Harold my address. How did he find out where I lived? Maybe he had tailed me on the way home.

Harold actually lived in the room on the ground floor of the same building and next to the staircase after mine. He was just too shy to come and find me. So he used his cousin to pass notes.

Mother soon found out where Harold lived. She greatly disapproved of his family. Too large, she said, too many siblings and uncles and aunties living together. There was also a sick and blind grandmother who slept on a bed outside their room. Mother warned me not to get intimate with Harold. Well, before and even after meeting Harold, I never ventured into that part of the building. And I was not at all curious about his family.

"He is also a Lee; remember, you cannot marry anyone with the same surname," she said. As if I would.

Mother seemed to view every member of the opposite gender who befriended me as a likely suitor I could take off with. I certainly had no such dreams about Harold. But I did not discourage his little acts of sending me notes.

Harold became my supplier of past exam papers. We were both studying similar subjects, so we would get extra sets of notes or exam papers for one another whenever we could. I can still remember the chemistry chart he bought and specially laminated for me.

It is memories like these—the card Harold bought from RI and posted to me, the letter he wrote to me while sitting in the open during the wee hours of his outbound camp—that I still cherish.

By then my school sessions were in the morning. Sometimes, when I was waiting for Uncle Ong, Harold would come hurrying by to catch the public bus to school. Often we would shout greetings or pass notes before our transport arrived.

This was the year of my GCE "O" Levels. Students were busy poring over their books. Even while waiting for transport they were going over their notes.

For me, all available time was spent on studies.

My siblings and I had grown up, and the room was getting cramped, especially at bedtime. Some enterprising carpenters came up with the idea of building a platform in the room. So my parents saved money, and had one done.

The platform spanned half the room. We could climb up easily on a small flight of steps. There were railings to protect us from falling off. Once on the platform, I could stand easily. My head almost touched the ceiling.

All the girls slept on the platform, while Heng and our parents slept below. A small table held all my books and a table lamp. I spent most of my time in this new bedroom, doing my studies and reading.

In the evening, when everyone was sleeping, I would read books or solve mathematical problems under the table lamp.

I needed more paper to solve the mathematical problems, but I could not afford to buy notebooks. Father often brought home discarded record books from the wards that I used as scratch paper. I would fill up every inch. Then, when I ran out of space, I took another pen with a different color ink to write over my scribbling. I had red, blue, green, and black ballpoint pens with me all the time. And I religiously solved all the problems at the end of each chapter in my textbooks.

Studying was very much a routine life. What was troubling was the tension I felt during exam period. There seemed to be pressure from everywhere to do well. Teachers often nagged us about getting distinctions[51]. One particular teacher even challenged us: "I can confidently say the RI boys will get eight distinctions. You RGS girls maybe can manage two or three." As for help, I didn't seem to get any.

Frankly, unlike many of my classmates who had distinguished parents, I was the least exposed to knowledge beyond the books. I

---

[51] Outstanding results—usually grade A or higher

rarely could get a copy of the daily newspaper. Besides school and library, I hardly went anywhere. So, it was no surprise I was among the average students in my class.

There were talks about the type of jobs we could get after the "O" Level Exams. Possibilities included teaching, nursing, and clerical services. I thought nursing would be a good choice, but Mother was against the idea. She said becoming a nurse meant I was superior over hospital attendants. I would be Father's superior. That would be intolerable for her. She also heard about girls my age going to the United Kingdom to train as nurses and never returning home. She was afraid that would happen to me, too.

Then Harold talked about going on to study GCE "A" Levels after the "O" Level Exams. Most of my classmates were also aiming to do just that, and I really wanted to also. So I mentioned that to my Mother. She did not make any objection.

Later I overheard her telling Father, "Your daughter wants to study Standard Eleven."[52]

So I went ahead and applied to study Pure Sciences in the same school. In those days, RI would admit girls for pre-university classes, but that year, the principal of RI refused to admit girls. We were puzzled. Anyway, RGS would be good enough for me.

But the first day at RGS for pre-university was a disappointment. Because of a shortage of teachers, the school had decided to change the subjects in the Pure Science class. The usual combination that included Applied Mathematics and Pure Mathematics was replaced with subjects like Biology. Mathematics was offered at a lower level. I was most alarmed. I relied very much on mathematics to do well, and I dreaded cutting up animal specimens.

---

[52] In those days, the Chinese referred to the class taking "O" Levels as Standard Nine and the "A" Levels as Standard Eleven.

My friend, Joan, immediately asked for a transfer and got a place at Beatty Secondary School (BSS), a boys' school. After consideration, I timidly asked for a transfer, too. But Miss Norris, the principal, refused to arrange for more transfers. It seemed she suddenly realized she was losing her students.

Then Joan informed me the teachers at BSS were very helpful. She encouraged me to apply directly to the school. So I braved the public transport and made my way to BSS armed with my school report book.

I arrived after the classes had started. A turbaned Indian man was at the notice board. I approached him timidly and explained my situation. He did not introduce himself. Instead, he brought me to his office and wrote a letter to Miss Norris. I got my place in BSS! Later I found out that he was Mr. Tharam Singh, the principal of BSS.

Miss Norris was incensed when I gave her the letter and gave me a sound scolding. But I was too elated to mind what she said.

Mr. Tharam Singh was a quiet and unassuming man. He certainly did not mind students like me joining his school. Unlike Miss Norris, he went about his business quietly. So, during the next two years, I hardly felt his presence.

There were only seven girls among more than twenty boys in my class. It soon became clear that I was cognitively stronger than most of my classmates. I was good at almost every subject, except General Papers. The lack of exposure to news and world events took its toll. But somehow I trudged along, gathering whatever I could from the teacher and my classmates. I even researched and borrowed all sorts of books from the National Library.

My strength was in problem solving. The Pure Mathematics teacher insisted that we attempt all the questions in the past exam papers. Each solution had to be written on a sheet of foolscap paper and filed neatly. We were to keep our files in the classroom cupboard in case we need to refer to them. I hardly referred to my solutions once they were done, but my papers became reference materials for my classmates.

To be appreciated like that was a big deal for a person with low self-esteem like me. I reveled in the attention I received.

The relaxed atmosphere at BSS certainly was much better than the competitive spirit at RGS. Every morning, I reached school early and strolled around the school field with Joan before class started. Although I never discussed my emotional problems with her, Joan's presence was a great support.

Eventually the results of the "O" Levels were announced. I managed a good enough aggregate of points to yield a Grade One Certificate. Father was delighted, although I was a little disappointed with myself.

News of my achievement soon reached Second-Auntie. She had a close friend who worried his son had no girlfriend yet. The prospect was a university graduate who was eight years older than me and working as an accountant. His father wanted to make sure the match had a good enough level of education. So the proposal came.

Mother was very excited—a rich man for her daughter! I resisted; I wanted to continue with my studies. As for Father, he said, "Not the same dialect, no good."

And so I was spared! Later, I often wondered what life would have been like had I ended up a tai tai[53] and maybe a lady of leisure.

Uncle Ong did not ply the route to BSS. So I had to take public buses to school every morning. It was always a rush. I would be at the bus stop bright and early to wait for the one and only bus service that took us to town.

---

[53] Rich man's wife

About the same time, Harold would come along. We took the same bus to the same point and went our separate ways. So we had more time to exchange news and notes.

What we discussed seemed insignificant now. I can hardly recall anything. But I really enjoyed those times with Harold.

Everyone was again busy preparing for the final exams—the "A" Levels. There was talk about applying for scholarships, particularly the Colombo Plan Scholarships. These scholarships were awards by overseas governments to study in their countries— Australia, New Zealand, Canada, the United Kingdom, and the United States. Joan and I were encouraged to apply.

Mother was upset when she heard about the scholarships. There was a lot of emotional outpouring and nagging. I guess she was getting more and more insecure since Grandfather had passed on.

I could not sleep well on the eve of the first paper for the preliminary exams. I was worried. So the next day I went to see a doctor at the hospital. The doctor gave me some tranquilizers, but that made it even worse. That night I did not sleep at all. The next day, when I sat for my Applied Mathematics paper, my mind simply couldn't work. I was so disappointed that I threw away the medicine.

Of course I failed my Applied Mathematics. That failing cost me the possibility of being nominated for the Colombo Plan Scholarships.

During the final "A" Level Exams, I withstood the nightmares and plodded on. At least my mind worked, and I sat through all the papers.

That incident with the tranquilizer was a blessing in disguise. With my regular diligence, even with a mind that was somewhat tired, I was able to perform well enough in the final exams. I topped my school and walked away from formal education with results that were quite enviable to my classmates, although a little disappointing in my personal opinion.

As soon as the exams were over, I started looking for jobs.

As for Harold, his final results were far from ideal. Despite all his hard work, Harold had frequent blackouts during preparation for the exams. He did not even sit for one major paper.

Being a male, it was compulsory for Harold to join the army and serve the nation for the next two and a half years. We had much less opportunity to meet. And then he stopped contacting me.

I lost a friend who had indirectly added much color to an otherwise insipid life. At the time I was sure Harold's male ego had prevented him from maintaining our friendship. But come to think of it, that might not be so.

Not long after I started work, the hospital administration offered Father a housing unit on another road behind the place where we lived. It was a flat with two bedrooms, a living room, kitchen, and toilet. We had been waiting a long time for it, so of course we moved.

Did Harold write to me or try to find me? I guess I will never know. Wherever he is now, I can only wish him all the best.

Chapter 18

Joining the Workforce

It was time to look for a job. The first thing I did while waiting for my exam results was to apply for the job of a relief teacher. I also tutor students. Some secondary school students came to my place, but they disappeared after a few sessions and did not pay me. I was too timid to venture out to provide home tuition.

Not long after my last exam papers, I was asked to teach in a primary school. The pay was eight dollars per day. At the same time, Rosie, who had just completed her "O" Level Exams, found a job in a factory. The pay was twenty cents an hour. This big discrepancy was a wake-up call for all of us. Betty, who had been drifting in her schoolwork, started to pay more attention to her studies.

Given our impoverished background, my parents were quite happy with the income I could fetch.

But Mother fretted over Rosie's pay. Rosie did not obtain a complete "O" Level Certificate. So she stayed on for a while in that factory job. Eventually, a friend of Mother's recommended Rosie to a Japanese firm. Rosie worked as an accounts assistant and went on to other accounts-related positions. Many years later she even became manager of an electronics firm.

It seems like Mother's children were equipped with good brains and an attitude for hard work. Our needs were for survival and safety only. A life of luxury was never in our worldview. We all led simple and frugal lives, and none of us ever landed in dire financial need.

For me, venturing out to work was another stressful adjustment.

I was posted to a school in Tanjong Pagar.[54] The children, mostly Indians and Malays, were from low-income families. I was the form teacher of a Primary Two class. Except for second language, I had to teach every subject—English, arithmetic, science, and even physical education.

Being unschooled in pedagogy, I crammed the children with as much knowledge as I could. But I dreaded physical education. The children simply ran amok, and I had a hard time controlling them.

I was also the only relief teacher in the school. Fellow colleagues were too busy to offer help or advice. The principal was a kindly old man. Once he caught me pulling the ear of

---

[54] An area in the Central Business District of Singapore, it was close to the harbor.

one student. He did not reprimand me. When I apologized, he just said, "You were stressed."

Finally, when the children took their midyear exams, I waited for the outcome with apprehension. The results: they did just as badly as the children in the other classes.

Being painfully shy, I felt terribly alone in the teaching job. Every morning I would go to the school with a heavy heart. I tried my best to prepare all the lessons beforehand and gave my best shot. But somehow I did not feel any sense of achievement. So it was a relief when I was finally offered a job in the civil service.

Mother was excited. A few days before I reported for work, she took me to People's Park[55] to buy clothes. Till then, most of my dresses were homemade. Now Mother bought me some ready-made ones. Miniskirts were

---

[55] The only shopping complex in Singapore at that time, it was a big cluster of stalls situated in the heart of Chinatown.

in vogue. I had both hipster-style and high-waist—the latest fashions in town. But they were Mother's choices. She bought me blue, brown, yellow, and green dresses but not red ones. She strongly believed red was not good for me—a fortune-teller had once told her I could become stupid if I wore red!

I was very naive. It had never occurred to me that I needed better clothes to wear to work. Mother had that presence of mind. The problem was she never taught me these things. And she bought based on her own taste. I just presented my body to try them on.

That was the only time we went shopping together for my clothes. Subsequently, I reverted to sewing my own dresses. Mother would buy materials she liked. I really had no say. So I did not get to wear red for a long time.

Now it was time to work! For twelve years I prepared to join the workforce. So I should have been prepared, right? Wrong! I was a green horn—awkward at socializing and most unpolished for work politics.

I was hardworking and zealous. I cleared my work every day. In the late afternoon before four thirty, dismissal time, my desk would be clean.

One day, while I was waiting to knock off, Mr. KC, my supervisor, came to me.

"What are you doing?"

"I am waiting to go home."

"Where are your files?"

"With the typists and referred to you for checking."

"And you have nothing to do now?"

"Yes, my work is done; I am going home."

"Look at your other colleagues; they are still working. At least you must pretend to be working."

It took me a long time to grasp this concept of pretending to work and helping colleagues look good. But it did not go down well with me. Some simply walked about, talked to one another, and carried over incomplete work to the following days. Assignment of new cases was based on the amount of incomplete work carried over to the next day. So some colleagues seemed heavily burdened. In reality, their output was low.

Also, some people seemed to get pally with their superiors. Others commented that they networked to gain favors and recommendations for promotion. Being that unschooled in human relationships, I really lost out.

The job probation period was three years. During this period, I had to sit for the departmental exams as well as the IM (Instruction Manuals) exams.

To prepare for the departmental exams, we attended lectures given by senior staff. Although quite boring, at least there was some help. But for the IMs, there were no classes or lectures. Most of the information was about procedures for duties I was not doing. To make matters worse, the documentation was complex and wordy. It was hard to comprehend and a big struggle for me.

I finally cleared my probationary exams and was placed on permanent appointment. In the meantime, I had been transferred from one division to the next to gain experience with more elaborate cases.

One day, Mr. KS, the deputy commissioner, called me into his office. I was selected to train for computer programming. But, before the final selection, I had to take an IQ test. I was elated. I had applied for such jobs in other statutory boards and passed the tests, but I was repeatedly rejected because my department's commissioner refused to "release" me. Now was my chance for a change!

I passed the IQ test, went for training, and finally was transferred to the division that had the computer!

The computer, a product of International Business Machine (IBM), was housed in a big metal casing. It was connected to a card reader and an impact line printer. Both were very noisy. Input media was eighty-column punched cards. So there was a supporting team of keypunch machines and operators, and a big, noisy card sorter. All these were housed in a computer room. To make myself heard amid the din, I developed quite a loud voice.

There were five programmers including myself. We used a programming language called RPG (Report Generator Program) to squeeze our logic into a computer with only eight thousand bytes of memory. It was a challenging job indeed. Our knowledge and experience evolved as we learned from our mistakes. To me, that was fun learning.

My work life had taken a branch up another career path. This path led to many adventures in learning and changes in work assignments. To the department, I was one of its pioneers in a new field. It was a career that spanned more than thirty years.

In the early days, there was more recognition for a staff of this nature. There was a strong belief that only people with great aptitude for mathematics were carved out for such jobs. So a left-brainer like me was greatly valued. And for the next few years, I was sheltered from office politics, as I concentrated on making the systems work well.

Chapter 19

Mother Again

One would think that with Rosie and me in the workforce, Mother would feel more secure. But she did not. She seemed to feel more anxious. She asked Father to make extra shutters for the main door and windows in the new flat. She had more aches, pain, and migraines and often doused herself with eucalyptus oil.

In the new place, without Chui Lian, she had nobody to confide in. Instead, she spent her time nagging us about housework not done to her satisfaction. Heng was growing up and becoming quite spoiled. But none of us could scold him. Otherwise Mother would find some excuse to get back at us. The tension at home was so bad that I rarely took annual leave from office.

Mother's problems seemed psychological. But being ignorant, I could do nothing.

Once I accompanied Mother to see a doctor. I ventured to ask him about her problem. She was complaining of itching among other things. The doctor did not confirm my suspicion about the psychological nature of her ailment but said she was very afraid during her hysterectomy. Besides a prescription for her symptoms, there was no suggestion of referring Mother for treatment. So, every one of us continued to live in a state of tension.

Suddenly, in the midst of my departmental exams, I developed rashes all over my body. So I went to a general practitioner near home. She told me I had German measles and cautioned me not to go near pregnant women. I was horrified. One colleague on my team was expecting a baby! So I stayed home until the rashes disappeared.

Not long after the rashes disappeared, my body started to swell. I saw the general practitioner again. This time, she said I had kidney problems and told me to go to the hospital for treatment.

The doctor at the Singapore General Hospital asked whether I wanted a quick or slow cure. I told him I wanted a fast one so he hospitalized me.

For the next ten days, I was injected with penicillin every six hours. Liquid intake and output had to be measured. The staff also monitored my weight. I had to get back to my normal weight before they could give me a clean bill of health.

The hospital stay was actually quite pleasant, except during injection time. Each time the needle was poked into my skin, I got an electrifying pain that paralyzed my leg for a while. Eventually I was discharged, and never heard of acute nephritis again.

I was too young to investigate the causes of my sudden illness, so I just continued life as normal when the symptoms disappeared. It was much later that I found out my autoimmune system could act up when there was too much stress in my life.

Mother blamed the Korean ginseng she cooked for me during the preparation for my exams. All along she believed I was born with a weak body. So she gave me "heaty" food.[56] On the other hand, she believed Rosie had a "hot" body. Rosie's tonsils often swelled, and she would develop a fever. So when Rosie fell sick, Mother would brew black bumblebees with black olives for her to drink.

Not long after my illness, Ben, a classmate at BSS, started dating me. He had completed his diploma course with the Singapore Polytechnic and was doing his national service in the army.

Two aunties around my age had boyfriends and were planning to get married. Kathy and Sally had long since married. So when I had

---

[56] Food that will keep the cold from the body

no steady boyfriend yet, Mother was afraid I would be left on the shelf. Still, she was disappointed with Ben.

I had no objection to him. We hit it off quite well. In addition to weekends, he made time to see me on some weekday evenings when he could get out of his camp. Only Mother was not happy because I went out too often.

She was so focused on getting me married that she did not realize Rosie was of marriageable age, too. The difference between Rosie and me was the boys from school visited and dated me, while none of her classmates ever visited her. For that matter, the same applied to Betty.

I now wonder if it was fear of incurring Mother's wrath that deterred my sisters from socializing with boys. If so, I must have been the bold one.

My episodes of migraines, bed-wetting, and panic attacks appeared frequently. I was ashamed of all these, but they were beyond my control. Mother's nagging could go on for days until I burst out. Then she would quiet down for a while.

Life was sometimes so miserable that I ruminated about the futility of living on. How could I get out of all this? As for Father, although he put up a brave front, I could see that he was upset, too.

I often envied friends and colleagues who seemed so happy. They socialized and partied after work. Former classmates were graduating from the universities and getting into lucrative jobs. Here I was bogged down in a most uncontrollable situation.

I explored the idea of moving out. But the thought of incurring more expenses stopped me. Half my pay went to Mother. The other half had to cover pocket allowances for siblings still in school, a small allowance for Father, my lunch, and the occasional outings. (Mother had all these carved out for me on my first payday.)

By the Chinese New Year, the little money I had managed to save would be used up for the celebrations. So I really didn't have enough money to rent a room elsewhere. Funny thing was it never occurred to me to cut Mother's allowance.

I often toyed with the idea of death. I thought of drowning, jumping, even taking pills. Eventually I told myself I could just jump when I could no longer bear it. In those days, high-rise flats were just sprouting up. We often heard of people jumping off them. The most famous venue was a block of flats on Pickering Street—the first high-rise that was eight stories high. That thought was comforting. I had a plan to get out!

When Ben came along, I changed my plan. I could get married and not come home any more.

But Ben had another year of national service, and financially we were not ready for marriage. We really had to wait. Mother was unhappy.

She insisted that Ben and I get engaged. So, although engagement was no longer in vogue, we went ahead with it.

*****

It was really a long wait for public housing. My parents were eventually allocated a three-room HDB flat. They were thrilled.

Of course, the flat was a bare shell. Mother engaged a renovation contractor to put in the flooring and tile the kitchen. Being a fanatic on cleanliness, she had the walls in the kitchen tiled right up to the ceiling! She said tiled walls were easier to maintain than painted ones.

So we moved again. Just about the right time, too, for not long after, Father retired from his job at the hospital.

And Mother's worries had been real. We could be out in the streets had we not applied for the flat.

Father was given a very small gratuity and a low monthly pension. It was just enough for his own expenses. But Father did not idle. He looked for jobs elsewhere. Given his experience in the hospital, he soon found a caregiving job. That took him away from Mother at least during the day.

Chapter 20

Free At Last?

Eventually Ben completed his national service and found a job with a computer company. We were overjoyed.

With Mother on our backs, we decided to marry and started looking for a room to rent. Second-Auntie found one for us in the block that she lived in—far away from Mother.

Ben's parents picked the wedding day and sent a matchmaker to find out Mother's requirement. Mother's demand was simple: ten dinner tables for her one hundred guests!

In those days, when marrying off a daughter, it was normal to ask for ten dinner tables to accommodate friends and relatives. I was not surprised with Mother's demand. But I was worried about the bills Ben and I had to foot.

And, of course, Mother would keep all the ang pows from her relatives and friends. Mother said she had to keep up with subsequent wedding invitations. That aside, gifts in the form of jewelry for the bride were also confiscated. The only item she did not take from me was the bracelet from Grandmother.

All these acts made Mother look mean, but it actually made sense for poor families like ours. Each time Father received an invitation, there was much worry about the amount of money he had to put into the ang pow. If the invitation was from a close relative, the bill would be bigger.

To save as much as possible, I sewed my own wedding trousseau. Mother bought most of the materials, leaving me without much choice.

Mother observed the customary obligations on her part. She bought bedding, a portable sewing machine, and other items—blessings for a happy marriage with many children. And she gave me the gold bracelets and necklace I used to wear during Chinese New Year.

In the days before the wedding, Mother was often tearful. She lamented that once married a daughter belonged to another family. I avoided her as much as I could.

One day, Third-Auntie took me aside. She said Mother told her I had been contributing to the family's finances. Now Mother was worried that I would cut that off.

Throughout her life, it seemed money was Mother's top priority. She worried about the roof over her head; she worried about losing a daughter—or was it a source of income or a lifeline? I kind of suspect the years under Japanese occupation took their toll. And her offspring and life partner had paid a big price!

Third-Grandaunt came bright and early on my wedding day. Following custom, she was invited to perform the hair-combing ceremony. She said a few good words, and then Mother and Father mounted the veil on me.

Mother was crying all the time as the makeup artist dressed me. I dared not look at her. I was afraid of breaking down, too. I wanted to leave as soon as I could.

Soon Ben, his best man, and my bridesmaids arrived. Relatives started coming, too.

Ben and I bowed to my parents and then at the ancestors' altar before we took the lift down to the car waiting below the flat.

I was feeling a little relieved when suddenly I saw Father and Mother waiting outside the lift door. They had walked down six flights of stairs to guide me to the bridal car.

I tried very hard not to look at my parents. "No, I must not cry. The false lashes will drop."

My feelings were all mixed. I was heading to a new life. Why must Mother make it so difficult for me?

Yes, it was going to be a new life, away from Mother and her control—my newfound freedom!

Three days after the wedding, Third-Auntie finally caught me on Second-Auntie's phone. "They all missed you. Rosie was crying when she spoke to me. You must go home."

Go home? Give up my newfound freedom? Hey, give me some space!

But Father expected me to return. Rosie, my lifelong co-sufferer, missed me. I was wanted at home.

Home! Where was home? Oh no, must freedom be so elusive?

Epilogue

The events in our lives happen in a sequence in time, but in their significance to ourselves, they find their own order... the continuous thread of revelation.

Eudora Welty

When Keith, my son-in-law, read the first draft of my manuscript, he was appalled with the ending. "You can't leave the reader hanging that way. He is sure to ask, 'What do I get after going through all this?'"

Dear, dear Keith, if every story ended happily, the world would have few miseries. The sad truth is, the living happily ever after that we found in fairy tales, rarely happens.

The flight from Mother led to many roadblocks. Just being a daughter had been so difficult. But being a wife, an in-law, a mother, and more couldn't be easier. In going through these life stages, many past ghosts often popped up.

Yes, unwittingly I carried the baggage with me. So what happened? Rather than write a lengthy account that could be boring, let me stop and leave the reader to guess. Maybe another day I might relate the sequel.

However, let me leave you some information to ponder.

Father died of a heart attack while watching a wrestling show on television. He was seventy-three years old. Mother died immediately after a colonoscopy. She was eighty-one years old. Both had autopsies done.

In the case of Father, the aorta dissected. For Mother, major arteries in the heart had burst. My conclusion: their hearts had been pounding too much and too fast.

It might be unkind to say, but the truth was, we, the children, felt released when Mother went. Most of us were already in our late fifties or early sixties.

Less than two years later, Heng, my only brother, passed on. He had third-stage cancer in the lungs, liver, brain, and many other parts of his body. He had been a heavy smoker and drinker.

Living under Mother's grasp had never been easy. But where did this tide of negative energy come from? Great-Grandmother, the Japanese occupation, or was it something beyond that? I am still curious.

About the Author

Lee Ali grew up during the difficult years when Singapore broke off from British colonial rule. Her parents were poor, illiterate Chinese raking out an impoverished existence.

About the Book

Lee Ali recounts her difficult years struggling under the stern discipline of her illiterate mother and the emotional turmoil resulting from the triangulation between herself and her parents. In relating her accounts, Ali gives vivid descriptions of Singapore before its modernization and the rich potpourri of food and culture of its pioneer immigrants. Many of the places described have now given way to development.